J.D. Netto's
Saved by the Page™

... VOLUME I ...

Saved by the Page ™ - Volume I
A collection of stories written by readers
who have been saved by books.

Contributors:
Alex, Abby Moeller, AlyMarie Fox, Amanda Hoyer, Ana Paula Camacho Pérez,
Annaellen, Ashlyn Cowart, Audra Fetherolf, Aurora Dominguez, Barbara Kljaic,
Bryant Dailey, C.A. Thomas, Charlotte Williams, Chaselyn Coats,
Cherish McKellar, Elizabeth Sagan, Elyse Reye, Emilie Messavussu , H.B.D,
Isabelle Armstrong, J.D. Netto, James Trevino, Jenna Van Mourik,
Jennifer Cazey Daniels, Jessica Lawlor, Jessica Shelley, Joanne Lumière,
Kate Birch, Katherine Sorensen, Kathryn M. Banks, Kendra Olson,
Krissu_LovingStories, Lilly, Laura Diaz Arce, Lynn Glass, Lynn Glass,
Michelle L. Villa, Nicole M. Bohr, Nini, Rey R., Shannon Rose Lee,
The Reader Myth, Ulysses Guerra, Yesenia M. Collado, Yessica, Zoey Allyn

Cover design © 2018 by J.D. Netto Designs
Book design and production by J.D. Netto Designs
Edited by Kristen Michelle

ISBN: 9780692184462 (hardcover)
ISBN: 9780692184929 (ebook)

dedicated to all misfits

C. W.   Sonia Egdi

James

Ann

Abby

Audra Letherlf

Sagan

A1

Lilly   J. Shelley   jenna V.

Melli & Mik   KS   K Jolie

Christeb M. Kellar   KrisWenu

JA   KmBanks

Bo Leyn   Kris

CONTENTS

Introduction

..J.D. Netto..

"But some day you will be
old enough to start reading
fairy tales again."

— C.S. Lewis

When I discovered books in my childhood, my perspective on life changed. Though only a kid, I'd look around and imagine life was a massive library crowded with packed shelves. Each book was a person, the pages filled with accounts of their every triumph and turmoil—hidden secrets, dreams, untold desires. Every period carried a purpose, every comma a breath. I used to tell myself that someday, someone would pick up my life's book, read it, and learn from it. The more I ran toward the written word, the more I recognized the truth in my imaginings.

At an early age, I was blessed with the privilege of going on book tours around the country after the release of *The Whispers of the Fallen*. Going to those events allowed me to meet thousands of readers. And amidst all that comes with book tours, what I looked forward to most was listening to their stories as they hung around the table. The majority shared deep tales of bravery and courage. But they'd always start the conversation by naming the book that changed their life. The more I listened, the more I was inspired.

At the end of 2017, while flying home from my last event of the year, a thought struck me: What if the readers got to write the book? What if it contained their tales of bravery and the salvation brought to them by reading stories?

The Saved by the Page movement was born.

I didn't look back. As the thought flooded my mind, I could see my younger self—a misfit rowing in the opposite direction of the crowd, following my own current. I recalled the times I turned to my favorite stories for courage and wisdom. And the more readers I met, the more I realized I wasn't the only one who found safety in books.

My honest desire is for this project to be a reminder that you're not alone. Somewhere, there's a reader going through the same things as you, fighting their own battles, and winning their wars.

May these stories remind you there's always hope. I don't believe in fiction. I believe fiction is truth written out in riddles, and those wise enough to understand them are changed as they go on their journey.

To those who entrusted me with these stories, I am forever humbled and grateful. We are about to change the world.

Beautiful Shards

..Zoe Allyn..

Someone once told me the shards of our sorrows get turned into something beautiful. I wasn't sure I believed them. Because those shards of mine, they haunt and control my life, day in and day out. How could my past possibly be beautiful?

When I was nine years old, I was sexually abused. As if that alone was not horrible enough, it was by a family member. Someone I had to see every day – who was trusted to be alone with me, who was supposed to protect and care for me. I don't know about you, but at nine I wasn't exactly up on my sex knowledge. I wasn't sure what was happening. I knew I didn't like it and I thought if I told anyone, I would get in trouble. I didn't know I was the victim. It went on for longer than I care to remember. It happened everywhere and anytime we were alone. While it was happening, I would block it out by trying to think of other things. I would count the seconds on a clock, how many fibers were in the rug, how long I could hold my breath, anything. Anything to not acknowledge what was happening. One day, while the unspeakable was taking place, my mom walked in. She was mortified, sad, angry, a mess. It stopped after that day. I took all the memories and stuffed them way back into the depths of my mind, behind a door with several locks, never to be opened again.

I thought I was fine. I really did. I still saw that family member every day, but he would pretend I wasn't there. I went on to become an honor student. I was in clubs and played sports. I was never the pretty one or the most popular, but attention wasn't my "thing." I had a nice circle of friends. I was fine. Up until my sophomore year of high school, when they required us to take sex education. I didn't think anything of it. It was just like any other day. I went in, sat down at my desk, and waited for class to start. Ten minutes in, I had tears streaming down my face. I got up and walked out. Everything I had locked away for so many years came rushing back. I couldn't walk. I couldn't talk. I couldn't breathe. All I could do was let the tears run down my face. Living through it once was awful. Reliving it a second time, when I truly understood and comprehended every little thing, was horrendous. I felt so broken and repulsive.

A few days later, I came home to a book sitting on my bed. *A Walk To Remember* by Nicholas Sparks helped me through the toughest of times. Showing me that while the sexual abuse I experienced was decided for me, it wasn't who I was. Showing me that I was not unlovable, that I wasn't broken. I related to Jamie in many ways. I didn't want people to know what happened to me. I went through my days quietly, unnoticed. As I read *A Walk To Remember*, I saw what love was. I saw the way Jamie's father loved her and realized my parents loved me the same way. I read as Jamie and Landon became friends and fell in love without realizing it, the same way I fell in love with the boy down the street. I was consumed by this book. It spoke to me and touched my heart in ways I never thought possible. I learned how to be a caring, selfless person from Jamie. Landon taught me how to take chances and stand up for what I believe in. Reverend Sullivan showed me how to be accepting.

I have since become an adult, and my shards no longer control my life. I still own *A Walk to Remember*. I still carry the lessons I learned with me. I reread it from time to time and, even though I could probably recite it from memory at this point, I always find a new lesson. It saved my life when I didn't want to live, and I will be forever grateful.

Fading Memories and Saving Books

..Lynn Glass..

It's a strange thing for me to be typing this out with no final plan. Even titling this came as simple words without any forethought. But that's the way things sometimes have to start.

The earliest "adult" book I can remember reading made a parental figure choke on an ice-cube, mocking me for spending hours alone in my room just watching TV or listening to music. A breaking point had come, and I pulled a paperback copy of *King Lear* from my backpack. That I was reading was not the shock. It was that I was reading Shakespeare.

I can truly say I did not have many friends. I was an only child. I was a loner. Quiet. Creative. Weird. And smart, although I refused to let that little bit slip out. And as the years passed, I read. Everything. I consumed books. The regular curriculum of junior high came, and I continued to read my own library selections featuring mythology, space travel, Atlantis, and all the fiction that

9

was popular at the time, alongside the required *Watership Down*, *To Kill A Mockingbird*, *The Cay*, and *Lord of the Flies*. Decades later, I can still recall them all.

There came a year in senior high that a small class was made available, where we could read a variety of books that were not the district standard. *Jurassic Park*, the first book of the class, had also just been released in theaters. We had to swear not to see the movie until we had finished reading the book. I read the entirety of it that week and was subsequently written up for not limiting my reading to the assigned chapters. That book was followed by Mary Stewart's *The Crystal Cave*. I didn't read ahead.

To balance my solitary literary consumption, I took a speech class at the same time. To this day, I can still recite the poetry works of Edgar Allan Poe that I had to memorize for the class.

The Crystal Cave finally came to a close in the literary class and the next author was named. I didn't know how much of an impact this book – this thin collection of less than 200 pages – was going to have on the rest of my life. It was then, I was introduced to the worlds of Ray Bradbury. More specifically, a 1992 paperback edition of *The Martian Chronicles*.

I honestly could not tell you what it was about this book that filled a hole I didn't know existed. I read the book over a weekend. Then I read it four more times before classes ended.

It didn't matter that the book was first published nearly 50 years prior to my discovery. I bought copy after copy as I found them; hard and softbound, each of a different publisher, publication date, and cover design. When the power would go out, I would grab my worn 1966 copy, sit outside, and read. It became my go-to when I needed to step away from things beyond my control and just exist. Then some publishing house decided to "update" a few now socially-questionable chapters and titles. I never bought another edition.

Slinking ahead a bit in time, it was over a year that I hadn't read a single book. It was a long time of personal trials and difficulties. My focus had been drawn to other things. But I didn't realize this until one day, while killing time, I walked into a used book store. The air of ancient trees and press ink instantly brought me back and the flood gates reopened.

I know pirates' histories and biological weapon patterns. I know pieces of dead languages and zombie apocalypse survival tips. I've learned about earth sciences and the bicameral mind. I found my religion. Discovered how things are made and how they are destroyed. I can see outside the box and both sides of the coin. I've read fan-fiction and 14th century porn. Criticized movies for ruining books. Learned the primer for speaking house cat. And I've traveled to meet authors and have them sign first editions.

Humans have an afterlife, that's why I seek out books published more than a century ago and rescue them from dark dusty shelves, letting them breathe in the open air again. I've found an endless love in pages because the older they are, the more cosmic stardust they've touched.

I'm still mostly a loner. Still quietly perched, watching the room. Creative. Weird. And still smart, although I let that little bit slip out more than I used to.

Never Be Ashamed
of What You Read

..Elizabeth Sagan..

I discovered my love for reading in 2007 and those have been some marvelous years. Until one day, when I decided I should stop reading my kind of books – books with magic and dragons and fantasy realms – and start reading "serious" books. I wanted to be a lawyer and I thought I had to kill the creative part of my brain since no one would ask me about Harry Potter, right? I was miserable. Trying to be someone I wasn't, trying to like things I didn't like. But in 2016, I had an epiphany.

Back then, I had stopped my silly experiment and had started reading like crazy again. And I asked myself, what can I offer to the world? My only talent, the only thing that made me different, what I had tried to kill with no results, was my love for pages. My love for books, for stories. And if I was feeling drawn to this world, to the book community, there had to be a reason. So maybe the pages didn't save my life, but I have tried to live without them and it didn't work for me.

Another World Away

..Kate Birch..

To escape to other worlds is to escape from reality. To travel to fantastical worlds is one of the best things about books. Even if they're based in reality, they can change how we interpret and see the world.

Books have always been one of my escapes into another world, another life. Living through the characters you're reading about can influence and change you in more ways than you think. Seeing something that could never be in real life; dragons, wyverns, hippogriffs, and much more are always a great thing to read about, to think of.

The darkness of the world becomes replaced with light, pulsating from the pages, brightening with each word you read. Letting go of the worries, strife, and tests people face on a daily basis – whether they be in the form of illness, disability, depression, anxiety – is one thing that is guaranteed from the pages of a book.

You're always welcomed into their world where prejudices against you are forgotten, and you, the readers, can finally have a place to be yourself and influence others.

Thousands upon thousands of stories are lifelines for people, giving them the ability to become more confident, unbound by social and ecological restraints that can separate people from one another. The feeling of freedom is more than anyone could think possible; there is nothing that a book cannot do.

For me, books have become a form of escapism. When I am tired of the world around me, when I feel like everything is against me, I dive into books and immerse myself within their worlds, their words – identifying myself through the characters and dialogue. Since I was eleven, I have always had a book with me wherever I went. And now, at twenty-three, my appreciation of books has soared past expectations and allowed me to branch out and read new material I never would have before.

Books are a necessity for so many people. Including me.

Books Are Sparks
of Light in the Darkness

..Elyse Reye..

Books are a spark in the darkness. Depression rots you from the inside out. First, it's a little voice telling you that you're not good enough. Next, you start to wonder if people are laughing or talking about you behind your back. Are you good enough? Do you matter? While we all go through these issues, someone with chronic depression, like me, hears those voices on a loop for eternity.

I have been depressed for as long as I can remember. Even as a child, there was a part of me that felt different, older, sadder than my peers. I smiled and laughed with the rest of them, but that small voice in my brain told me I wasn't smart, pretty, or fun enough. Frustration found an outlet in perfectionism. If I only got it just right, I might prove myself worthy. No one understood why I so desperately felt the need to prove myself, why I cried in bed at night. I lived two lives – one, as a wide-eyed and precocious child, who took on each challenge with enthusiasm. The other was my internal life, the endless monologue that ran through my head day-in and day-out. Every day was a struggle to maintain my upbeat façade, and it was exhausting. Emotionally, mentally, physically – I wore myself out. The harder I tried to keep all the balls in the air, the worse it got. I needed an outlet, a way to shut my mind down and relax. At the time, meditation wasn't readily accessible in my community, and prayer just wasn't right for me. I tried everything until, one day, I picked up a book I hadn't read in a few years.

I climbed into bed after a long day and opened the book to the first few pages. I read through a couple chapters lazily and knew I should have stopped, but, for the first time I could remember, my brain was completely focused. The words on the page became pictures, the scenes enchanting mini-movies that were playing just for me. I saw another life, far away from my small and cramped surroundings, where anything was possible.

The voices were silent.

They weren't nagging me about not being good enough or telling me everyone hated me. Books liked me. Books only wanted to be read, and they loved me because I wanted to be devoured by their stories.

As I passed through the teenage and college years, I clung to my stories like a lifeline. I took so many literature classes, I accidentally ended up with a second major. I worked in the school library just to cradle the worn, cracked spines and smell the musty old pages. I crammed for exams in the study room, giggled in whispered tones with friends, and found new literary loves all in the same place. Books sustained that inner life of mine, allowing me the quiet and sense of peace I normally lacked.

Until 2013.

That's when I dropped the balls.

Rather, they fell and knocked me on my rear end. I have a complicated medical history, and in the beginning of that year, a new medication caused me to get critically ill in a matter of days. The next few months were a blur of hospital stays, new treatment plans, failed recovery, and unimaginable pain. I'll spare you the details. When I was finally released from the hospital, I couldn't walk on my own. I didn't speak. I didn't move for hours at a time and needed to be reminded to take care of basic needs. I was spoon-fed for a week. It wasn't a mental break, not exactly. I wanted to talk and engage with the world, I just couldn't. Some days, it felt like being trapped in my own body. While I could communicate, I still wasn't fully present. We tried binge watching my favorite television shows and listening to my favorite bands. Nothing woke that spark in me. I hadn't found the thing that would connect me to the world.

Then came my old friend, the book.

In hindsight, I don't know how my husband and I didn't think of it earlier. Out of the blue one afternoon, I noticed a book at my side. I picked it up and, since it didn't require movements that induced pain, flipped through the pages idly. It was a light-hearted Latinx romance, nothing that would tax my brain. The dialogue was light and snappy, just the way I like it, and I laughed at a solid one-liner. It wasn't a loud laugh, barely more than a puff of air, but it was the most emotion I'd shown since my return from the hospital. From then on, new books filled my bedside. I devoured them, connecting to the characters in a way I couldn't connect to people. Dragons rekindled my adventurous spirit. Shapeshifters made me want to venture out into the night. Sweet romances invoked the feelings of falling in love all over again. I began to feel. And once I could feel, I tentatively expressed myself. Day by day, the more I read, the easier words flowed from my lips. One night, over a game of Uno, I laughed for the first time in a month. Then I smiled. I read before I got out of bed, in the park, and in waiting rooms. I chatted about what I was reading with my physical therapist as she patiently taught me how to walk again. The depression was ever present, probably at its strongest, but reading was the only time I experienced true relief.

Those hours I spent reading were as vital to my recovery as anything else I did. I spent a lot of time in fantasy worlds, living through the *Dragonlance* series and their many offshoots. I feasted upon Harry Potter and came to love the deep, dark recesses of the minds of supernatural assassins and thieves. Just as I filled my outer life with activities that reconnected me to friends and family, I filled my soul with those words.

Something curious happened. Stories formed in my head. Characters sprang to life and demanded to be set into action. I tried to ignore the urge. I'd never written fiction. I had just stopped working. Writing stories was for other people, not me. Feeling more foolish than ever, I opened up a blank document and started typing. Words flowed from the wee hours of the morning through the evening hours. Within a year, I'd written two exceedingly bad novels with no real plot. They rambled. The characters swore too much. My world-building was terrible. As one of my earliest readers told me, it was like the dialogue happened in a vacuum. I was so proud of myself and, although I'm glad I never published either, felt so alive. After months of scribbling and butchering the English language, I'd created worlds in which someone could lose themselves in, the same way I'd always lost, then found, myself in books. That was magic.

Five years since the days that changed my life, three years since I felt that magic, and here I am. Reading and writing have become everything to me. Not a night goes by that I don't fall asleep with a book in my hand, and not a day passes when I don't write. My depression isn't gone – it's something I'll struggle with for the rest of my life, but I now have a way to beat the system. I write for fun, and now professionally. I've published three urban fantasy books for the same reason I keep picking up my favorites time and time again – I want fun, exciting, sometimes scary worlds to lose myself in. Now, I get to take people along for the ride, and, hopefully, give them a minute of respite from the stresses of their lives.

Fighting for Air and Stability

..Nicole M. Bohr..

For every book I read, I make sure to thank my aunt. Why? Without her, I probably wouldn't be living life. You see, ten years ago, I was fighting to survive. I was twenty-one at the time and had lost over forty pounds in less than seven months (without trying). Pain riddled my body (doctors could not find a cause... yet) and depression started to set in. Thoughts would creep in that maybe I was going mental. Was the pain all inside my head? Was I imagining it? Thankfully, I found a doctor who would listen and was treated for a tumor in my ascending colon.

After a few complications, I was stuck in the hospital and received a get well package from my aunt. Inside the box were the first two novels of Janet Evanovich's *Stephanie Plum* series and some toys. My initial thought at seeing those books was not positive. I knew my aunt was a reader, but me? HA! But, since I had nothing to do, I said, "Why not?" They were just books and who knows, maybe I'd enjoy them? Well, not only did I enjoy them, I fell in love.

When my family and friends heard that I enjoyed reading those novels, everyone pitched in to buy the rest of the series. I will be forever grateful. Those books helped me escape the situation I was in. I would stay up late at night giggling in my room, my nurses telling me to get some rest because it was three in the morning. But how could I sleep when I couldn't put the book down? Umm, hello Ranger! That book helped me escape reality – filling me with joy and laughter.Ten years ago, I finished my first novel that wasn't a school assignment. Ten years ago, with the help of my aunt, I fell in love with reading. Since then, my aunt has introduced me to a couple of Minnesota authors (John Sandford, Julie Kramer) and, of course, they did not disappoint.

One for the Money will always be my treasured item, and I am eternally grateful for my aunt.

Thank you, aunt Shari!

Finding a Light

..Isabelle Armstrong..

Everyone has something. We all have life challenges that shape and define who we are. For me, it was my autistic brother. Recalcitrant fits of rage and holes in the walls were my norm growing up. From the unhealthy living environment I found myself calling home, I developed severe anxiety and depression. It was not uncommon for me to hide away in my room for hours, praying the screaming and hitting would stop. In those long stretches of time, when the walls seemed to close in, and I felt like my tiny world was collapsing, I would desperately reach out for anything to keep me stable, any small distraction from the hell raging on around me.

In those dark hours, I stumbled upon a light. Small at first, the tiny spark grew to a fierce blaze that I now identify as my burning passion for the written word and literature. Books consumed my life from the age of five on. From stumbling through the learner's books of *Dick and Jane* to lugging around *Deathly Hallows* in the third grade, earning incredulous looks from my teachers, my love of reading grows each year. Books have helped me work through the trauma that comes out of abuse and find strength in overcoming my mental health struggles. Whenever I would have an anxiety attack or the words "You'll never amount to anything" spewed at me, I would find solace in the arms of my favorite characters, like Harry Potter, the boy who lived, or Feyre Archeron, a woman who thought her scars would never heal.

Books are the most beautiful form of expression humanity has to offer because it allows us all to hear the message this world is in such desperate need of: You are not alone. Without the companionship books have given me, I would not have been able to escape the cold grasp of suicide and find a way to dance out the healing joy I find myself basking in today. Books are much more than ink symbols stamped upon tree carcasses. They are unity. They are strength. They are light.

From Nightmares to Salvation

..Michelle L. Villa..

Sharing my story is very difficult because it's something I have tried, for years, to ignore and forget. I was eight years old when the stories between the pages of books began my path towards salvation. My early years were not filled with happy family memories; they were more like nightmares. We lived in Mexico from the time I was three years old until I was eight. And while we were there, a side of my father came out that I never could have imagined. He became very violent towards my mother; I tried to stop him on several occasions only to be held back by family members who feared that I would also be hurt. As the years went by, it only got worse. When we came back to the States, my father's abuse turned towards my siblings and me. I might have taken on more beatings, being the oldest of five with one more on the way, because it felt like it was my responsibility to protect my family from my father. On many occasions, I thought I would be at peace if maybe I just didn't exist anymore. I tried taking my life so many times, but I would look over to my five siblings and think, *Who will protect them?* At the same time, I felt that if I didn't find an escape from my reality, I would lose my mind or that, one day, I would not stop myself from committing suicide.

I said I was eight when books started my path towards salvation because that's when I was introduced to the school library and discovered *Goosebumps*. A series that gave me the escape I needed from the nightmare that was my life. When I was ten, my sixth grade teacher gave me a book she thought I would love. Of course, seeing that it wasn't *Goosebumps*, I refused to read it. To this day, I tell everyone she tried to push this book on me because she was tired of reading my *Goosebumps* book reports. She kept insisting I would love it, so I finally gave in and opened up the book that would save my life both physically and mentally. That book was Harry Potter!

We all know the story of the boy who lived, but I never imagined that same story would help me be the girl who lived. Harry Potter gave me an escape and J.K. Rowling saved my life. As the years went by and I waited for the next book to be released, my life did not, by any means, become easier. I was taken from my parents and placed into foster care where I would endure five years of mental abuse, but I stayed because my sisters needed me. During those years my mother abandoned us, we were left with only two options: stay in foster care or move back in with my father. Even if my father had done everything the court asked him to, I would still have chosen foster care as the lesser of two evils because I could never trust my father again. Books were my escape from that reality. And in those books, I traveled to unknown places of magic and adventure. My salvation all goes back to books because, without them, I really do not believe I would be here today.

And since I love reading so much, that same year I was introduced to Harry Potter, I started writing my own stories. I am not published yet, but I hope the possibility is in my near future. My biggest dream is not fame and fortune, but that one day I can save a life the same way mine was saved – through the written word.

From the Darkest of Pits to the Brightest of Lights
..Kathryn M. Banks..

For three years of my life, I was looking into the deepest of pits and seeing nothing but the infinity of darkness staring back at me. Nobody really tells you how mental health can change or control your life. I didn't understand until it happened to me. I had been a reader since I was a child and was always able to occupy myself between the pages of a good book. But when I went to university, the agoraphobia I'd been battling since my early high school years overtook my life with a vengeance. I lost interest in everything I loved; I couldn't even bring myself to step onto the train to get to school most days. I lost myself.

On one of the rare days I actually made it to university, I was passing Waterstones on the way back to the train when a book in the window caught my eye. It was called *Finding Audrey* by Sophie Kinsella. Its cover showed a girl with big sunglasses, standing in front of a backdrop of green and yellow stripes. I have no idea why the book stopped me in my tracks. It was obviously contemporary and far from the typical books I would read (I'm a total fantasy lover). I went in, picked up the book, and bought it without finding out what it was about. When I got on the train, I started reading it and was astounded to find that it featured a girl battling with the very same things I was facing every day. I finished the book that night.

Finding Audrey became an obnoxiously green and yellow striped bright light that began to bleed into my consciousness every time I felt the darkness trying to overtake my head and stop me in my tracks. It pushed me to pick up another book, to see if I could replicate the pocket of sanity and safety that *Finding Audrey* had created. I started to read at least three books a week, the words running together, occupying my mind, and becoming a safety net that stopped me from falling back into the pit of darkness that had been my home for so long. Reading didn't just help me find myself in the characters I fell in love with, although that was how my experience began, it also taught me that I could become who I wanted to be. I read about characters who started out lost and found themselves through heartache, challenges, and seemingly impossible odds. Reading showed me I could conquer whatever was standing in my way, that whatever I was facing wasn't an enemy, it was a part of me I had to learn to embrace before I could step forward.

Reading might not have literally saved my life or 'cured' me; I still battle for my sanity every day. But reading gave me a life

I could never have imagined. It helped me finish my degree and start writing again. It gave me back my sense of self and connected me with hundreds of people around the world who love the same things I do. My love of reading was kickstarted again by that candy-stripe cover in a shop window. It allowed me to continue my story in the light of a world of possibility and opportunity that, without the thousands of words I have read since that day, I would never have seen was right in front of me.

Harry Potter
and my Angel

..Aurora Dominguez..

I remember being in college at the Universidad del Sagrado Corazón and walking into Plaza Las Americas in San Juan, Puerto Rico after a tough college day to enter the, still existing, Borders bookstore. My uncle, Angel Aguilar Jusino, and I were meeting for a movie and some coffee, and he ended up purchasing *Harry Potter and the Sorcerer's Stone* for me as a gift. The rest is Hogwarts-based history for this Hufflepuff.

I grew up on the ethereal tropical island of Puerto Rico and my uncle was my hero. Not only did Harry Potter save me that day, with its captivating story, but my uncle did as well, just as he'd always done whenever I had a bad day or didn't believe in my writing or my talents. Thanks to him and his inspirational ways, I became a journalist, and now a professor and a teacher. He believed in education and made sure we discovered new gems by subscribing us to magazines, such as *Rolling Stone*. Books were his life, he instilled a love of reading into the hearts of my cousins, my brother, and me. I still clearly remember that day we saw the first film together and how much we truly enjoyed it. After that, I continued reading the series that has now become a pop culture gem.

My uncle passed away from pancreatic cancer in February 2018. His spirit and love for us is eternal. I think of him whenever I read about Harry, Hermione, and Ron and watch the films. Thank you, Angel. I will remember you and your love for reading. No matter how much time passes, I will always be grateful. Always.

How I Stayed Strong

..Nini..

I started reading because I have dyslexia, and the extra reading was supposed to help with my tempo. I never disliked reading, but it wasn't really my favourite thing at that time. My aunt owned lots of young adult fantasy books so, by the time I went to high school, I had found my genre.

From the first day of high school till the very last (even after I changed schools), I was badly bullied. I didn't fit in with the popular crowd, nor did I ever try, and I started to feel really lonely, spending more time in the school library than the cafeteria.

My love for books grew and grew in those days. The special escape a fantasy novel provides is one I have found nowhere else.

The nightmares where I got ripped apart slowly transformed into magic-filled dreams full of faeries, vampires, werewolves, and many others. After a few years, and lots and lots of books, I start-ed adopting some of the good traits of female characters. It was nothing major, more the "How would she deal with this?" type of thing or my personal favourite: "I am Celaena Sardothien and I am not afraid." This gave me a lot of confidence.

In those years, with few friends and little to do, I found a haven in books – a place to just be me without having to withhold a part of myself, be quieter, less noticeable. To this day, even though I now have friends whom I love dearly, I always carry a book to feel safe.

I've Seen Worlds

..Kendra Olson..

I can't lie, I've had an incredible childhood. I am a lucky person. I have never had to worry about money, my education, or my ambitions. But my life is not perfect — no one's is. When I moved overseas before kindergarten, I didn't know what to expect. I actually thought Switzerland was a fake or imaginary country. Our mom raised my sister and I as readers, and we spent every night before bed reading together. That was how we connected.

When I moved back to the United States in fifth grade, I experienced more culture-shock than I could have imagined. My life was spent driving to Italy or France on long weekends, going to school with people from around the world, and experiencing more as a seven-year-old than most do in their entire lives. Northern California was a bubble to me. So I went back to what I always knew: reading. I discovered books like *The Hunger Games* and fell in love with dystopia. I made friends because of reading, and it was the greatest time in my life.

We then moved to New Jersey. It was unexpected, and I was heartbroken because I had made such wonderful friends and I didn't want to leave them. So I chose to isolate myself a lot. I threw myself into books like never before because at least it was something. I fell so deeply in love with characters and immersed myself in their worlds in order to feel like I was a part of something. Seventh and eighth grade were some of the worst years of my life. I chose to become someone who didn't believe in themselves, giving in to my anxiety and depression and anything negative in my life. I finally started going to therapy and had to get a psychiatrist. The number of times I tried the unthinkable in the past five years terrifies me each day.

In October 2014, I attended my first New York Comic Con. The first panel I went to was on a Thursday night and it was, mostly, so I could see James Dashner. *The Maze Runner* books touched me so deeply because I had never related to a character more than Newt. But it was that same night, I got to hear Pierce Brown talk for the first time; I was 13 years old and picked up *Red Rising* thinking that my mom would like it. That series changed my life. For the first time, I was getting to follow a series from the very beginning, and being a part of things from the start made me feel special. I don't know what made it such a profound story outside of the obvious reasons (plot, character development, etc.). Something about Pierce Brown himself resonated so deeply within me that when my mother met his mom, they talked about how on earth children with such deep imaginations and worlds in their heads can be raised. I sent Pierce a message about my experience with his books, and I'll never forget what he told me: "… that hope is already inside of you, books just help to bring it out."

I have lived in worlds and I have lived in bubbles. Books were the only sources of real life for me as a third culture kid. No one I have met has shared my life, aside from my family. It is so hard to connect to teenagers who have lived in one place their whole life. Who have always had the same friends. Who have never been a part of more than one culture. I am indebted to literature and can never repay them for the worlds I have traveled to.

Just a Little Bit Personal

..Lilly Santiago..

The first book I ever recall reading and loving was *Gratefully Yours* by an author whose name I cannot remember. But I do remember how that book made me feel and what the rough yellowing pages were like between my fingertips as I turned the page.

The last book I recall reading and loving, I was nearly nine years old, and life had finally taken its toll on me.

There's a common misconception the young cannot suffer because they haven't experienced much of the world yet. And while I do believe some of that to be true, some pain can only come with age and experience, I have to say that, for being so young, I've seen my fair share.

There was no mistaking that ever since I was young, I was different from the other kids. Not in a way that made me an outcast, but in a way that drew people's attention and often left me feeling confused. I was smart and beloved by all my teachers but, when it came to being on the playground, I was a wanderer. I didn't have a group of friends to sit down with and talk to. Yet, in class, I got along with everyone. Being older, I now identify that feeling of being alone on the playground as sadness.

Middle school was a completely different experience. I'd blossomed into the social butterfly I was destined to be, but there was always a whisper in the back of my mind that something was wrong.

I had read many books before; the *Percy Jackson* series, *A Series Unfortunate Events*, *The Hunger Games*, *Matched*. But the book that shaped me into the woman I am today was *City of Bones*. I'd come across that book during a particularly difficult summer that was a turning point in my life.

I was thirteen years old and had ordered the original trilogy. I practically devoured them as I sat by the windowsill on my favorite beige couch – quite literally one of the only pieces of furniture in my apartment. If you opened up that book, you'd see a long silver thread woven through the pages where all of my memories from that summer have been stitched in. And if you reached into my chest to pull out my heart, it'd probably be in the shape of that book.

My mother had lost her job that March and, the month before, my father had threatened to take her to court for custody of me. A threat that came to fruition one summer evening as I was scrolling through Cassandra Clare's Tumblr, and she came into my room, sobbing, to break the news.

Things began to deteriorate from there.

I threw myself into my reading. Whatever I could get my hands on. I brought a new book to school every day, not because I'd gotten bored of it, but because I had finished it the night before. Reading was a way for me to escape my problems; my mother's growing drinking problem, the bills piling high on the kitchen counter, the lack of food in the fridge, the calls to the office when I was behind on school tuition. These are all things I've kept to myself for so long but never dared to voice aloud or even put into writing. I'm not sure why.

It isn't anything I'd share with the adults in my life, either, because I know they'll say I'm lying. And it's not because they think what I'm saying is fabricated but because, deep down, they know I'm telling the truth. And they're probably ashamed that a child had to grow up at such a young age.

I feel like that sometimes. Like I grew up before my time.

We ended up losing our apartment and we moved back into my grandparents' house – my childhood home. My mother remained unemployed for years to come, the court battle was stressful and scarring, and I was living in such a toxic environment. I felt myself drowning over and over again but didn't even know it.

I threw myself into the literary world. I wrote my own novels and was sure I'd found my calling. Bookstagram and Booktube were just starting, and so I occupied myself with those things. I started going to book signings and formed a book squad when – When for the first time in my life, I decided I wanted to die.

It was perhaps a month or so before my fifteenth birthday, and the first time I whispered the words aloud, I felt shocked. Terrified. I took those thoughts, shoved them to the back of my mind, and tried to ignore them, but I couldn't. I started scouring the internet for answers. I took every one of those "Do You Suffer From Anxiety and/or Depression?" quizzes I could find. I think, in the end, I took around fifty in total. I realized I needed help – to tell someone. So I told my mother.

And it was a mistake.

I told her I felt depressed and that something was wrong. I even showed her my test results, and she ignored them. She told me I was self-diagnosing myself. That there was nothing wrong with me and maybe if I did something with myself, like left my room once in a while, I might feel better. "Fresh air," she said, "is good for you." At the time, I didn't know how to speak to her. I was too young and uninformed to know that what I should've said was, "Isolation is not a cause of depression. It's a side effect."

I finally told my doctor and she sent me to a therapist. I only went for around two months before I couldn't go anymore. My mother had no job and, one day, she forgot to call and cancel the appointment. The cancellation fee was too much for her to pay, and nothing else in the area was covered by our insurance. If we even had insurance.

I can't remember much of those details.

At sixteen, I tried to cut myself for the first time. At seventeen, I wrote a last will and testament because I planned on going home and killing myself. She laughed it off and put the paper in her folder. I didn't think she believed me, so I kept putting it off.

Every once in a while, I'd tell her, in specific detail, what I wanted in the event that I died. I'm sure she wrote it off as nothing more than my twisted sense of humor, but I made her promise. And she did, even though she wasn't fully aware of what she was promising me.

I got my first job at a bookstore. It gave me purpose. I could escape from a toxic home environment, and it gave me something to look forward to while I was miserable at school, in yet another toxic environment. That job was my escape. I had so many ideas I would share with my manager because, originally, I was brought on to help appeal to the YA audience in NYC. It fell through after a wrongful termination that, at sixteen years old, I didn't know how to deal with. But that's okay.

Because one day, when I'm an internationally bestselling author, they're going to wish they had treated me better.

For the first time in my life, I felt like I could open up to people. I'd met great friends through all of my bookish shenanigans, and I didn't feel like an anomaly anymore. I was able to accept my therapist's diagnosis of severe depression without telling myself other people had it worse and I had no right to be sad. I could tell them about my growing anxiety, how I'd self-sabotaged in school, distancing myself from my other friends and my church. All the things I couldn't tell the adults in my life, I told them. We shared our stories, and I didn't feel so alone.

That has been my greatest problem in life. Always feeling alone.

I was on top of the world. I concealed my depression and anxiety like an expert. I no longer wanted to take my life because I finally had something to live for. Every story in every book I ever read played a part in saving my life. One way or the other.

But then, I crashed again.

I lost my friends. I was expelled from school because I didn't want to go anymore. I stopped reading and writing and doing all the things that made me Lilly. That vibrant butterfly, that bookish NYC socialite, the girl with the flower crowns and the eyeliner just vanished. Somewhere along the road she died, and I let her.

And I don't know why.

But I'll let you in on a little secret. After many (failed) attempts at writing this story, a very good friend of mine came to NYC for a visit. We spoke, went to church together, and he told me about this passion project we've been talking about for months – Saved by the Page. He asked me why I never wrote my story and I said, "I've written it a thousand times and I hate it. It never comes out right."

After we parted ways, he left me with a lot to think about. The day after, I cleaned up my bookshelf for the first time in months. I went through my old bookstagram account and old photos from little miss socialite days. I realized I lost myself somewhere along the way, so now I'm sitting down to write my story. Because I know there are many of you out there like me.

I wish I could fit every detail of my journey into these few pages but there will be other times to share different stories. Today, I've tackled one. And there will always be tomorrow.

* * * *

In the weeks following this visit, I picked up a book for the first time this year. I didn't finish it, of course (I didn't have the time). But I felt that spark in my chest. The kind fourteen-year-old me used to get, only this time it was different – older.

I wrote something down for the first time in a year. I bought books at Barnes & Noble for the first time in a year. And I started to do it again – to pick up the pieces of my life. But, this time, they'll be arranged differently. It's okay to reinvent yourself so long as you're able to find who you are in the end. No matter where this goes, wherever the path of life takes me, I'll walk that road with a book in hand. Because it's my lifesaver.

And I'm sure that if you're reading this right now, it's your lifesaver too.

Little Did I Know

..Chaselyn Coats..

I've always loved the idea of books. I've always loved that new book smell. I've always had a knack for reading and writing, but *little did I know* how much of an impact it really made on me. When life became unbearable, cracking open my favorite book and escaping reality, for a brief moment, always made it all okay. I would sit on my couch or in my chair for hours simply escaping because a made-up world was where I wanted to be. The more I read, the more I wrote. Today, I aspire to be a successful writer. Books help with anxiety and stress. Books help with sadness. Books save lives. Our messed up world needs a little bit of inspiration on the pages of its book. Get out there and create your story.

My Soul Is an Inkwell

..Amanda Hoyer..

I'm a writer-in-the-making, but not without first consuming the lifeblood of my imagination – myths. These multigenerational, multicultural tapestries feed my dreams, waking and sleeping. I began with ancient deities before moving to modern mythical beings of the cape and tights ilk, wherein I found my calling of meaning-making through myth.

I started with the Greco-Roman pantheon, where I lamented with Eros over foolish Psyche; flew to the highest heavens with Bellerophon and Pegasus; tragically fell with Icarus; and dreamed of becoming star stuff like so many fallen heroes. I traveled southeast, where I dwelt among dusty tombs of ancient rulers. I languished in sun and shade with the retired warrior turned protector, Bastet. I soared over seas of sand on the back of Horus. I fell in love with the Library of Alexandria and mourned its murder with Thoth. I weighed my heart on Anubis' scales against the Feather of Truth and found myself worthy. Eventually, my ka departed to a New World, where I learned of tricksters like Anansi and Coyote.

When I outgrew my childhood friends, I began questing for my significance in this life with Arthur and Merlin. I did not desire to slay dragons, but to befriend and understand these beasts. Little did I know, I was learning to tame my own inner demons at the time. In dreaming of riding dragons, the writer in me first awoke. I saw these beings as misunderstood, twisted monsters who needed someone to speak for them, helping them and the world understand why their fire-breathing was a byproduct of pent up rage and agony. I wished I had the magic of Merlin to save the day for myself and my friends. But alas, this was not so.

So I started writing. I realized that words were a power of mine and I could do incredible things when I put pen to paper. Nothing could stop me – save myself – from exercising this grand ability. And then my brother introduced me to superheroes. I had viewed some cartoon adaptations before, but nothing compared to the actual graphic novels in my hands. We consumed these stories by the omnibus. Weekly issues were certainly not enough for our voracious appetites. These stories kept me close with my brother during a time when I had no one else. I began developing depressive tendencies from fifth to sixth grade, and my brother had no clue as to the heroic way he was there for me.

I kept writing throughout all of these stories, pouring my feelings onto paper. Although my family was present, I never felt like I could really tell them what was on my mind. The "best" part of depression is not wanting to burden others with your pain, as you might feel shame for not being "normal" and happy like everyone else seems to be. High school involved lots of teen literature with strong female heroes, angst, and romance, which did not do much for my need to "fit in" with the self-perceived normies at my school.

It was not until college that I realized why myths and superheroes spoke to me in the way they did. It was not about escaping into other worlds, the magical abilities or powers, nor mere childhood nostalgia. I finally recognized that these were the stories of people explaining their world, naming their tragedies, overcoming the boogeymen of the unknown, and persisting through their trauma. I realized these narratives, whether explaining why the universe existed or how to deal with tragic origin, were because some storyteller sat down and dared to define the world. In no uncertain terms, these people pulled from the deepest, darkest unknown to produce the richest ink and record stories that have lasted lifetimes. These storytellers dipped into the inkwells of their souls, defining the inexplicable and establishing an ultimate power – they are the writers of their own fate; they control the words on the pages of their lives. Just like me.

One Book at a Time

..Ulysses Guerra..

I wasn't always an avid reader. In fact, it took me a long time to pick up a book I actually wanted to read. Before I picked up the book that changed my life, which I'll get to in a minute, I had read a couple books for school, you know the ones that you were forced to read and annotate for weekly grades. The ones that seemed so boring until you go back, read them years later, and realize you made a mistake by not paying attention in class.

Although I wasn't much of a reader before, I have always been an avid writer – from a short story of a cat named Cat to a full on 300+ page novel many years later. I loved writing so much that it started to anger my parents. My mom would clean one part of the house, move on to the next, and by the time she returned, the floor would be covered in pens and notebooks with all sorts of writing in them. Sometimes that writing didn't even make sense.

My mom had a bookshelf in our living room, but if you were

57

to ask me how many times I opened one of those books, I'd have to be honest and say none. That is until, one day, I laid eyes on a book with beautiful green letters going down the spine. Intrigued, I opened it and began to read. The first two words of the first chapter made a light turn on in my head: "Harry Potter." When I read those words, I recognized the name from kids in my class talking, nonstop, about this boy. I kept reading and finished the book within a day. It wasn't till I really looked at the spine that I realized I had made a mistake, at the top was a beautiful green number three. At that moment, I realized I had started the series with its third installment. I looked over our bookshelf to find the first two, but only found book four. I walked up to my mom and begged her to buy me the first one and, eventually, she did. Seven books and five sets of them later, I've grown an obsession with Harry Potter and the amazing world J.K. Rowling created.

After finishing the series and watching every possible J.K. Rowling interview, sometimes more than once, I decided the little boy who wrote stories about a cat named Cat wanted to become an author. I rummaged through our notebooks and found an empty one with pages ready to be written on. Seven years later, I had a 300+ page book. I still look down at the document and thank J.K. Rowling for, not only opening the world of books to me, but inspiring me to write my own and one day become a published author.

One Page at a Time
..Bryant Dailey..

I am and always have been a person who doesn't altogether fit in anywhere. Mostly because of circumstances out of my control and my own values of right and wrong.

Here are some things I was never fated to do which, ultimately, made me harder to understand:

• An athlete was never an option, really. As per my parents' wishes, I attempted to follow in my brother's footsteps by trying out baseball. But I decided sports, in general, were a no-go for me after running from home to first base.

Why did I give up so soon? Simple. I had severe asthma that was out of control. The run from home to first left me so out of breath, I needed my inhaler. Two puffs later, I decided to forgo baseball as I did not feel comfortable participating in something that could induce an asthma attack.

• Acting was not in my cards either. My only appearance in

this field was as an oversized duckling in my elementary school's production of Charlotte's Web. I looked cute, but the fun soon came to end when I started constantly ripping my costume.

• And, finally, singing was NEVER in my future. Sure, I am human and enjoy singing because it's fun. But I could never take these pipes of mine to Vegas. I sound like a mixture between a dying goat and frog whilst singing. (Don't believe me? I promise to send a snippet upon request.) Also, I generously want to ensure everyone's eardrums stay intact.

Around 2008 is when I started immersing myself fully into the glorious realm of literature and discovering all the beautiful things it had to offer.

Ever since then, I have changed for the better by learning I can fit in more.

Books have saved me so many times. 10 times? No. 100? As Eleanor Shellstrop from *The Good Place* would say, "Oh, fork no!" 100+? You bet your sweet barnacles.

Here's how:

• They helped me find my best friends who are always there for me through thick and thin. Find yourself a friend who reads. If they don't, send them to the Chum Bucket.

• During my junior and senior year of high school, I developed a truly special friendship with my librarian. Every time she was placing orders for a new shipment of books, she would ask my friend and I for recommendations. We would write down our suggestions and be the first to check out the new books to let her know what we thought!

• My tenth grade English teacher saw how much I loved books and how much they inspired me. She encouraged me to try and write my own stories. And I am so thankful for her because that's how I discovered my love of writing.

• Books helped me stay away from things my peers found to be "cool," such as underage drinking and smoking. Reading has shown me the consequences associated with indulging in those destructive behaviors.

• I learned that being unique is truly special and beautiful, especially living in a world that tells us we need to act and dress a certain way.

If I go on any further, I'll end up with a ten page paper in the dreaded MLA format. However, I want to talk about the most essential way books help me.

Books allow me to escape my life, especially when everything around me is coming untethered. They allow me to step into a character's shoes and see how they rise above their troubles and decide to keep on swimming, instead of sinking and succumbing to their sadness and pain.

I try and equip myself with their strengths and experiences to overcome my own demons. Sometimes I luck out and succeed. Most times, not so much. But at least I tried. And I'll try and try again until I'm successful.

This is my perfectly imperfect story. Filled with ups, downs, and everything nestled in between. But hey, that's life for you.

I do not own a T.A.R.D.I.S., therefore, I cannot change the past.

I can, instead, choose to grab the reins that control my life. Embrace my downs by turning them into accelerant to fuel the fire burning beneath my feet to shoot for the stars and achieve my dreams. Even if I feel like the fire is burning too hot and turns me to ash. I will rise again from the ashes like a phoenix and burn brighter than ever. Just like all of you exquisite witches, vampires, elves, or whatever else your beautiful spirit takes the shape of.

Openly, Honestly Me

..Alex..

Ever since I can remember, I've lived in some type of shadow. Maybe it was my older sister's shadow, my mom's, my friends', or even the shadow of my own expectations, but it's always been there. I was hiding behind a mask I had created for myself. I was the smart, quiet guy. I had friends, I was perfectly average, and I was lonely. I was lonely because I wasn't myself. I was playing a character in a story I should have been writing, but books changed that. *Paper Towns* by John Green, *Openly Straight* by Bill Konigsberg, and *Aristotle and Dante Discover the Secrets of the Universe* by Benjamin Alire Sáenz are the books that saved my life.

Paper Towns taught me that sometimes people are just people. They are not ideas or stories, they're just *people*. I needed the reminder that I was a person, not an expectation. *Openly Straight* taught me I shouldn't be ashamed of who I am, and that I shouldn't try to be something I'm not. I didn't need a mask to live a "normal" life, I just needed to be me, whoever that was. Ari and Dante taught me not to be ashamed of what or who I loved. Love is more powerful than whatever shadow I may be under, even if that love is self-love. Books gave me the chance to remove the mask I had made, become the author of my life instead of the supporting character, and see there is nothing else I can be than openly, honestly me.

To whoever reads this, even if you don't like to read (which is totally okay), don't be afraid to be openly you. You are the author of your own story. You are not alone. The mask is not forever. Go forward and love whatever and whoever you want (especially if it's yourself).

How the Shadow World
Saved Me

..H.B.D...

This story is personal and not meant to offend anyone.

I've been poor my entire life. Homeless three times. My mother's side suffers from alcoholism and drug use. And both of my parents have struggled with substance abuse; one of them still does. Things were never great at home because of this. When I was seven, my mother almost drowned me while she was drunk. Since then, I've almost drowned six times. My parents would fight a lot too. Then my mother started taking her anger and hurt out on my sister and me. My sister would take most of the beatings.

As life went on, I started struggling with my sexuality. It became a lot. I felt so... lost. Then I read Cassandra Clare's *City of Bones* and got wrapped up in this other world. I related to Clary's fiery personality, Izzy's distrust, Magnus' wisdom and freewheeling bisexuality, Simon's terrible jokes, Alec's honesty, and Seb and Jace's pain. I gained confidence in who I was because I was so inspired by those characters. And now life is a little better because of it.

The universe Cassie made is more than just a fictitious story (I mean, it may not be and all of us mundanes just don't have the Sight). It has real emotions and world problems expressed through abstract metaphysical means. It's full of both deep meanings and hilarious content. If I hadn't gotten into reading, I would probably be this small, quiet girl with no friends, feeling alone and scared. But now I have a network of close friends and a girlfriend who means the world to me. And I hope to create change and make the world better.

I would like to thank everyone who reads this, it means a lot to me.

Queer, There, and Everywhere

..Katherine Sorensen..

I have always been bookish, and my childhood summers were fueled by frequent trips to my local Barnes & Noble and watching *Full House* reruns on ABC Family. Not a bad way to spend a summer.

Okay, okay... the *Full House* reruns may be a tad questionable.

It was the summer before my freshman year of college, during one of my routine trips to Barnes & Noble, that I came across a book in the Teen Fiction section titled *Kissing Kate*. I was immediately intrigued by both the title and the cover design. Upon reading the synopsis on the back, I realized this was a book about a lesbian romance. I suddenly found myself becoming even more intrigued, so I bought it. Little did I know, this book was the start of something big. I spent my entire high school career purchasing and rapidly reading any LGBT themed young adult novels I could find. Through the aid of those books, I was able to come to the realization that I wasn't so different from the girls in the stories, and I took comfort in the fact that I wasn't alone. I gained the confidence to come out to my family during college because of the few, but brave stories featuring young LGBT romances. I am out and proud because of literature, and it's a beautiful thing.

Reading Books
Literally Saved My Life

..C.A. Thomas..

My story is kind of traumatic. I am autistic and, unfortunately, I had quite an abusive father who loved to mess with my mind by acting nice one minute and hating on me the next. That, coupled with my autism, just messed up my mind even more than it already was. Reading books had never occurred to me because, *back then*, I thought reading meant sitting in a chair for hours and staring at words printed on pages. That didn't appeal to me. What did interest me was getting out of my house, far away from my father, so I could escape the bullying and act like I didn't want to end my life. But it wasn't just in my own home that I was being bullied and abused. In high school, people I didn't even know – and who didn't know me – would do the same.

During that time, I'd always wonder what I was doing wrong. Why were people bullying me? What did I do? Back then, I kept thinking, "Is it that I exist that people hate me?" To this day, I still don't know why people in school – again, people *I didn't even know* – would bully me, but bully me they did. Their words kept bringing me down until I felt like I was trapped under the weight of it all, and believe me when I say that weight felt like a thousand bricks lying on top of me. I had no strength to pull myself out and no one around to give me a helping hand.

I was massively depressed and in a very dark place when I picked up *the book*, and the only reason why I picked up *the book* that day was because I was grounded. At that time in my life – when everything changed for me – my mother finally had enough of being abused by my father, and she'd kicked him out. I did something to anger her and, as punishment, she grounded me and took away the Wi-Fi. Then my sister decided to add salt to the wound by taking away the cable leads to all TVs in our house.

This terrified and angered me because whilst I was stuck in my house alone with no Wi-Fi or TV to distract me, I only had my mind to keep me company. That was a very dangerous thing for me. I was actually scared to be left alone with nothing to do but think, and just when I was about to have a panic attack with the voices in my head getting louder the quieter the house seemed, that's when I saw *the book*.

Both my mother and sister were reading it since it was all the rage at the time, so I decided to give it a go. Want to know what book it was?

Fifty Shades of Grey by E.L. James
Now don't judge me on my choice of reading. I had no idea

what the story was about, nor did I know what to expect from it, but it was *something* to do that would hopefully keep me occupied. So I started reading Anastasia Steele and Christian Grey's story.

I think it was maybe a few hours later, when I was halfway through the book, that I realised everything was quiet. I was reading this book, completely hooked, and *my mind was quiet.*

Actually... **Quiet**.

I couldn't hear my father's voice in my head shouting abuse at me; I couldn't hear my own self-doubts; I couldn't hear the girls at school calling me a whale and every other mean name in the book; I couldn't hear *anything*. All that was on my mind was Ana and Christian's story. And I cried when I realised that.

My whole life, I've been looking for noise to drown out my own thoughts; I don't think people realised just how much I wanted that noise to stop. I sought it out because of the voices in my head, but all it ever gave me was a headache.

Quietness is what I really wanted, and reading books gave me the quiet I've always craved.

I still think about this story – MY story – a lot. Once upon a time, I was ready to end my life because I was in a very bad place – a very *dark* place – and I saw no light at the end of the tunnel I was stuck in. Heck, I'm pretty sure I was facing the wrong direction and just kept on walking to the back of the tunnel, drowning in that darkness because it was all I ever knew.

But now? Sure, I'm still in that tunnel, but I can see the light I've always been looking for. Reading quiets the voices in my head telling me to turn around and go back, to just get lost in that darkness again. Getting *lost in books* is what has those voices slowly going away because, for a while, I'm not living my life – I'm living someone else's. And I'm going on one hell of an adventure where I'm either finding love in the most epic of ways, saving the world with the magical powers I wield, or solving a mystery that no one but me can solve...

Reading books literally saved my life, and for that, I will be forever grateful.

Reading Helped Me Escape from Grief

..Jenna Van Mourik..

I had always been very close to my grandma. She was one of the most important influences during the formative years of my life. We shared a love of the same things, mainly, classic books! Going to Grandma's house was always a treat because she would often tell me the story of Anne Shirley in *Anne of Green Gables*, or read to me from *The Secret Garden* or *Little House on the Prairie*, until I fell asleep in the little fort she always allowed my cousins and me to make in the middle of her living room every time we visited. It was because of her, that I first developed a love for stories.

I would become so entranced with the books she used to read with me, that they would quickly become all I could think about. Like all grandmas, she only encouraged this love of mine, producing craft projects related to the books and helping me make costumes out of old clothes so I could pretend that I was Laura Ingalls and Anne Shirley.

In my middle and early high school years, I had a falling out with reading because, according to my social group, it wasn't "cool." I was told I needed to focus more on my social life, social media, makeup, and clothes. Then very suddenly on one hot, summer morning, my mother received a call that changed all of our lives.

My grandma had suffered from what the doctors' thought was a stroke. They were doing everything they could to help her and had transported her to the nearest hospital that specialized in that sort of thing. Only when she got there, we were informed it had not been a stroke at all. My grandma had an aneurysm in her brain, and there was nothing that could be done. The week after her death was a blur, family had been coming and going in and out of town, our refrigerator was overflowing with pasta salads and casseroles from good-natured neighbors and friends. People would say things like, "Are you doing okay?" and my entire body would fill up with hurt and anger. Of course I wasn't doing okay! I wondered why no one understood what I was going through. I had just lost one of my best friends, one of my closest family members next to my parents, someone who I considered my "kindred spirit."

One day, I suppose my mother saw the blank, empty, sad look in my eyes, and suggested that I try reading something to take my mind off things. At the time, I thought she was being ridiculous. How could reading do any good? Reading certainly couldn't bring my grandmother back, and stories had always been something the two of us shared. It didn't feel right without her.

My mother, persistent in her own loving way, handed me a book and told me I had to read at least fifty pages. If, afterwards, I wanted to stop, she would never ask me to read again. I remember the book vividly – the vibrant green spine, the way the thin pages creased and crackled with every turn. That story was my escape. I was once again entranced by the worlds, the characters, and the wordy descriptions in each paragraph. After that, I never stopped reading. In time, I even found myself smiling and laughing again. After a year or two, I was able to reread *Anne of Green Gables* without crying. Reading helped me go from grief to joy.

I think it was because of all those stories my grandma shared with me, that I inevitably became a writer. One day, when I publish my first book, it will be dedicated to her memory. For without her influence, her love of stories, and her encouraging love for me, I would not be the person I am today.

Reincarnation, Dance, Rebirth

..Joanne Lumière..

"When I'm sick of the sky,

when I want to yield to the ocean,

who's gonna catch me when I fall?"

    Luhan - Catch Me When I Fall (2016)

"A paradise of survival."

That's what my life has been for the past few years.

We all feel pain and loneliness. Through the suppression of our environment, we get depression. Life begins to fall apart. A "melancholic unreality." Trapped in a bird cage, unable to crawl out, as we watch our life descend into madness.

The pressures of education in an Asian environment, through the last few years of high school, was a descent through the eighteen levels of hell to the very depths of despair. I remember those days when I cried and cried, because of school and not being able to catch up to the curriculum, because I was feeling useless, because I felt betrayed by my friends. I've asked myself the following many, many times:

What is the meaning in life?

Why must we keep going?

Isn't it better to simply...end your life?

I pondered death for eons of seconds. The pain and consequences I would bring upon those around me, the price I'd pay to leave this world when so many others desired to live, the cost of living in an environment — where the environment itself might as well be the cause of death — just to see the world out there.

Then, I found my first answer.

They say the strongest form of chains that anyone can wield are words.

I found the power to hold me back in books.

In the infinite stories and worlds, through every page and sentence, and by every single author. In the beauty of the language they weave, the stunning sceneries of real-life places or lands of fae, the glimmer of intergalactic worlds, the radiance of light and hope in each and every character. It was an escape, my magic of resurrection, a spell to keep me going further and further. I would forget about reality and dive into those worlds as the girl I aspired to be, fall in love alongside the heroine, go on an adventure to the end of the world, heal my scars, accept the past, and reach out to the future.

Knowing there are so many book characters who have also

been through a dark past, makes my journey even more reassuring. We share something in common, and that is why I am able to understand them, to listen, to find my own answers as they find theirs.

But, sometimes, it wasn't enough.

When no one around you understands the worlds you've seen, when there's no one you can truly share your emotions with, you hide all your deepest, darkest secrets. You hide your fear and despair from your family and friends because you will still be left alone when the darkness envelopes your heart and keeps the bird locked in its cage. You search for an anchor to hold on to. Something other than the reaching hands of words or the imaginary friends you've been talking to since fourth grade.

And then, I found my second answer.

I turned to the next page of my story.

And found the people behind the stories.

Authors, bloggers, fan account owners, cosplayers – a whole new community of people with similar worldviews, who spend their time lying on couches until their bottoms go numb from finishing a story in one sitting, people who fangirl about book characters because they're hot and sexy, people who share their connections with books and how books saved their lives as well. Book conventions and events, author signings, all these different places where people gather to meet and talk to each other, share the stories they love along with their personal stories. Living all the way in Hong Kong, it seemed impossible that I would ever attend one of these events. But I was able to meet an author who visited Hong Kong during her honeymoon; I went searching high and low at a mall after my mock exams and managed to meet her that evening, as well as a very kind BookTuber attending VidCon, whom I met up with on a late Saturday night during my university tour.

There are no coincidences in this world, only the inevitable.

Our encounters were inevitable. I promised those wonderful people I met, and I promised myself:

Just wait a little longer.

Until you can see them again.

We are the ones who cheer them on and give them the motivation to continue creating magnificent worlds, universes, and characters. Despite the distance of over twelve hours by plane, they wouldn't want to see me disappear from their world so soon either, and they became my motivation to keep going.

So I held on.

I waited and counted the days.

Every time darkness took over, I searched for that last spark of hope and held on to it for as long as I could.

I was granted a wish.

In 2018, I was fortunate enough to attend BookExpo and BookCon upon my graduation from high school. There were so many wonderful people of imagination and understanding, people I'd never met before, that I finally got a chance to talk and connect with, people that weren't "infected" by the toxins of competing over grades and universities, people who had a much greater heart. I met the masterminds behind the greatest of pages – the books that became my anchors tethering me to mother Earth. They were all wonderful and not one of them made me feel the loneliness that had been eating my soul away for years.

It was the happiest I'd felt in a very, very long time.

It was true joy.

I know there are more worlds to discover.

More characters to encounter.

More authors who create these universes to meet.

I escaped the reincarnation of sadness from adolescence,

I danced in joy as my heart continued to beat,

I treasured my paradigm of rebirth,

knowing that like a phoenix rising from the ashes,

I was saved by the page.

Send Out
the Message
..Jessica Shelley..

Battered and bruised from emotional turmoil, I finally escaped the fog of confusion to search the shelves for others who had shared my experiences and lived to tell the tale. But, unfortunately, I found nothing. There was not much guidance for children or teenagers who had suffered from emotional abuse. My only healing was through possibility. Through fantastical worlds, I clung onto inklings of hope; a magical wardrobe, a faraway tree, a wizarding world, a guidebook filled with secrets. Through stories, there was more to the world than it seemed – people who defeated their personal dragons and found themselves at the end of the journey. Reading that was like finding a little bird on my shoulder. The one Dickinson had called "hope." It said, "You are not alone, even if you feel like you are. Keep holding on. There is a world you have not discovered yet. Freedom and opportunity will come when you least expect it." I waited for my Hogwarts letter and received it when I had the chance to leave my world behind and start afresh at university. But it took a long time and a lot of healing. So again, I turned to books – pages chock-full of wisdom.

It is vital there are books in this world that can offer that to children. Especially the seekers.

I'm in the middle of taking a year off of education (Creative Writing MA) to chase my dreams by writing a YA myth-inspired fantasy novel I will be querying at the end of the year. Without books, I never would have had the strength to do so. I hope my stories and future writing projects reflect what I needed when I was younger, so that others do not have to scavenge the shelves and come up empty. Through experience and fantasy, I believe, is the most powerful and connective way to do this – to breach the abyss of souls, heal, give hope, and start a kindling of courage. So one day they may start a fire within themselves, grasp the letter of opportunity, and start a new, untainted adventure full of possibility.

Stories are messengers, stepping stones, matches, gateways. Each book is a little feather cupped in the author's hand that they softly blow away like a message in a bottle, gently passing on their insights and guidance to others.

So as Jungian psychologist, Clarissa Pinkola Estés, says, "send out the message of our return to those who are like us." For who knows who may answer the call and find a pack of wolves, just like them, with an entire wood waiting for their bounding feet. Which, in turn, could spark a flame of courage to write their own story and pass it on.

Stories Were My Downfall and My Road to Recovery

..Cherish McKellar..

I hated reading. But my mom forced me to sit down and read for half an hour every day. I was stubborn and spiteful to her because of it. But soon, a love for reading caught fire.

I always had a story playing out in my head. I would sit and imagine myself as a fairy, escaping and flying away from the bad guys. I was young, in seventh grade, and as I grew more curious about life, so did my imagination and my ongoing stories. As time went on, the internet became a substitute for my "stories" that were no longer so innocent. And because it was so easy, I fell prey to porn and didn't even know what I was watching. But once I started, it was impossible to stop. No matter how hard I tried.

I would cry myself to sleep at night, thinking I was a disgusting and horrible little girl. Porn controlled my life. My grades started to fall because porn took up all my time. I was at the will of my laptop.

My reason for staying quiet about this demon I couldn't control, was fear. I was afraid to tell my parents because of the anger and disappointment that would inevitably follow if somebody found out.

This continued for a considerable amount of time.

Until my dad found my secret. And I was free.

The road to recovery was not easy. Not in the least. Porn doesn't stay on the computer. Once you've seen it, the images and videos seem to be branded into your mind. I was afraid of myself and of computers. I couldn't be alone with my own mind without watching a replay of all that I'd seen. What I no longer wanted to ever see again. I wanted to be DONE.

So I started reading again. The time and freedom from my porn addiction rekindled my love for stories and fairies. In the pages of my books, I was safe. The courage of the characters strengthened me, showed me I could fight, and taught me I am more than my past mistakes. I may have scars where nobody can see, but I also have a secret power; at any moment of any day, I can become someone else. All I have to do is open up a book, and I am gone from the world that makes porn so easy to stumble upon. Away from my own mind and into another's. Into someplace filled with magic and adventure.

It has now been years of freedom from my porn addiction. And though time has healed me, it was books that really saved me.

- C.J.

Time to Fall
in Love with Life

..Shannon Rose Lee..

I first thought about killing myself when I was twelve.

Mind you, it was more of a passing thought than an actual suicide attempt. I remember thinking "I can always kill myself" as if it were the solution to a problem I had yet to uncover.

Twelve years later, I now know the problem was depression, but back then I thought it was normal to feel the way I did. After all, the characters in the books I read were apathetic, moody, and constantly considering killing themselves, so who was I to question it? I was ill-equipped to understand and process the emotions I was finding in the YA section of the Borders bookstore I frequented.

I found life to be increasingly dull and predictable. Each day, it became harder to get out of bed.

That is, until I discovered an unsuspecting book called *Twilight*.

To say that *Twilight* consumed my life between the years of 2006 and 2012 would be putting it mildly.

My bedroom was covered in posters; I had the Edward action figure, the snap bracelet, the band-aids...

Twilight gave me more than fictional men and women to fantasize over; it gave me a reason to look forward to living when I was deep within the abyss of my undiagnosed depression.

First there were the books, for which I forced my parents to drive me to the store on release day or to a midnight release party filled with giggling teenage girls and stupid activities, like "Draw Bella's Wedding Dress." Then came the announcement of the films, and the Twilight Tuesday videos from the set, and the magazine articles, and the DVD release parties.

To say that it kept me alive is an understatement.

To say that it is a massive part of my life, to this day, is an understatement.

I fell in love with the story, but *Twilight* also gave me time to fall in love with life.

It made me want to become a writer so that I, too, could weave stories that bring hope and meaning to others. It gave me a shoulder to cry on and a world to retreat into when the outside one became too much. It gave me friends even when my depression was pushing everyone away.

Which is why I will never doubt the importance of books and storytelling, and why I will always wear my Twihard badge with pride.

To Read or Not to Read

..James Trevino..

A lot of people read because they want to escape their daily problems, if only for a few hours. I think I do that too, but to an extreme degree. Because I feel so ridiculously trapped and limited by this world, to the point where I have this question I ask myself every single day: If a magical portal opened before me, would I jump in knowing that one, I might never get back, and two, I don't even know what's on the other side? Most of the time, the answer is yes. And it's so crazy to think that way because I am blessed with a pretty good life and I am grateful for it. But at the same time, I always want something more. And that's when reading comes in to save me.

Escaping Reality for a Moment

..Yessica..

Books saved my life. When I was first diagnosed with anxiety attacks, I felt alone. I felt ashamed and embarrassed. I felt like I was going insane. No one around me could relate because no one else had it. People told me that everybody gets anxiety, and everybody gets overwhelmed. No one could understand the pain I was going through.

My doctor told me to take up hobbies that would distract my mind from itself, so that's why I decided to start reading more often. And I felt myself gaining strength from the characters I read. It helped me cope with anxiety – to accept and deal with it. I was not going to allow anxiety to control my life and everyday actions because, with anxiety, you fear everything. Just plugging your phone into an outlet, you fear it. Turning the stove on, you fear it. It was hard. But reading helped me stay grounded, kept me from going insane, from feeling alone. For that, I appreciate authors because they have no idea what their writing does – what their writing is capable of doing.

When All Hope
Seems Lost

..Jennifer Cazey Daniels..

At the beginning of last year, my world came crashing down around me. My mum was diagnosed with stage four small cell lung cancer. The doctor's prognosis gave her one to two years to live. I know none of us are immune from death, but to have an estimated timeframe makes it even more terrifying. Suddenly, I felt as though I had to make every single second count because the window of time I had with her was narrowed. I've read countless books where characters deal with situations like this and I wanted to be one them, because at least they got through their tragedies and hard times with a nicely resolved ending. Maybe they found love along the way or discovered their true destiny. There had to be something more to all of this, right? And what I wouldn't give to skip ahead to the end and see what was going to happen. If only life worked that way. The book *A Court of Wings and Ruin* had just been released before my mum was admitted to the hospital for a procedure to start chemotherapy. To say I am obsessed with the *A Court of Thorns and Roses* trilogy by Sarah J. Maas would be an understatement, but suddenly I found myself having a really hard time reading. I was processing the words and turning pages, but I couldn't retain or engage with the story. I almost considered putting the book down and giving up. Have you ever noticed how your reading habits often dictate what you're going through in life? At that time, I wanted to just lie down and give up. I wanted to believe in a happy ending where everything would be okay when the last page was written, but what if it wasn't? The weight of reality was far too crushing to imagine going forward. Everything I loved felt like it was about to be taken from me and I was powerless to save it.

I went to work before my mum had her procedure and I was having a hard time focusing on that too. My manager walked over to ask how I was doing and how my mum was. We shared simple small talk. Then he said, "You're a writer and a reader. You have this kind of hope and optimism within you that makes you believe, at any second, a dragon could fly down from the sky. That hope you find in stories is what will get you through this, because anything is possible." Once he said that, I realized he was right. Stories had given me this unique hope for life and a belief that anything truly is possible. And while I might not get a flying dragon, maybe this part of my own story would be for something far greater if I could just see it through.

I'm not a quitter. I will read a book I don't love just for the sake of finishing it. And I suppose that same quality applies to how I live my life as well. I don't quit, no matter how much I sometimes wish I could. I like to believe it's my faith in God that keeps me going, but whatever it is, I had to push on through. So, I continued reading *A Court of Wings and Ruin* even if it meant me rereading a page over and over again until I made sense of it.

The day of my mum's procedure, I was sitting in a very crowded hospital waiting room feeling anxious. I remember clutching my book as if it were the only lifeline I had to keep me grounded. I sat there for hours reading about Feyre and Rhysand going into a battle they weren't sure they could win. For Feyre, it felt as though she was going to lose everyone she loved and the world she knew was going to vanish. At times, she felt powerless and hopeless, but she refused to give up. As I sat there reading, I began to find myself engaging with the story again, because it felt like I was in Velaris alongside those characters. I was terrified of what was going to happen next but knew I had to push forward no matter how hard it got. At one point in the story, Feyre had to take a great personal risk, and she did so because her love for Rhysand, her friends, and family, was far greater then herself. In that scene, she was confronted by her own demons and fears, but remembered being told, "Only you can decide what breaks you, Cursebreaker, only you." That line gave me goosebumps when I first read it, but seeing Feyre fight her own darkest self and conquer it made me feel the impact even more.

Sitting in that hospital waiting room, I reminded myself only

I could decide what broke me, and this was not going to be it. I was capable of getting through anything and, just like Feyre, I would fight till the very end.

The day before my Mum began her first round of chemotherapy, I had that quote tattooed on my arm. That way we both could look at it and be reminded we weren't powerless. We had the power to choose what would break us and what would happen next in the story of our lives. I look at my tattoo every day and it brings me hope that whatever the end of this story might be, one thing is for certain – I'll never give up. Don't stop reading just because life gets hard. Don't let the world tell you "it's just fiction" because to us, it's hope. Books are more than an escape or just great stories, they are a guidebook for life and they remind us, like Feyre did for me, that we are the authors of our own lives and the legacies we leave behind. So, what will yours be?

Words on a Blank Page

..Ashlyn Cowart..

I fell in love with reading at about nine years old, and my passion for it has grown every day since. But it wasn't until 2015, when my best friend killed herself, that I found the true power of reading. I was in such a dark place for a long time; I did not know how to cope with all that happened. Then one day, I picked up my copy of *The Complete Works of Edgar Allan Poe* hoping to lose myself in the pages, but I did more than that, I found the light I needed to get out of the dark. When I was reading through the poems and stories, I came across "Annabel Lee." The way he loved her, the way he grieved, and the way he was able to continue living after losing someone he loved so dearly, showed me that I could too. It showed me that others had felt this pain, and I was not alone. If he could lose the love of his life and still get up every day, then so could I. I will always be grateful to Edgar because I truly believe, without him, I would have given into the darkness. I will never forget the day I was saved by the page.

Beginning, Middle, End

..Jessica Lawlor..

A book is a story you would never know if you didn't take the chance to read it. You would never be able to experience someone else's thoughts. To me, reading is not about finding a good story, it's about connecting to each book, character, place, or relationship. It's the ability to get lost in a book and imagine a whole other world, knowing that it is totally different than what anyone else is thinking. Reading makes me feel, create, and imagine only what my mind can see. It lets me know I'm not alone, that yes, some people feel what I feel. Someone out there is going through something, just like me. Reading is a part of me and, without it, I'd be lost.

Characters Gave Me
Back My Inner Strength
..Audra Fetherolf..

I ended an abusive relationship through the confidence I won back from characters in a book. I was always an outspoken person and thought I had too much self-respect to wind up in an abusive relationship. Until I did. It wasn't immediate; it was little things over time until I just lost the will to keep fighting, making me more and more submissive to him. I started to lose myself. Family and friends, who got the rare chance to see me, often said things like "I don't recognize you" or "You never smile anymore."

When my daughter was born, things became so much worse. My ex had to get up early for work which meant we needed to be quiet while he slept. With a newborn baby, that is extremely hard to do. I spent every single night keeping myself awake so if the baby cried, I could take care of her without him waking. I would spend those nights, weeping silently, wondering how I was going to get us out of this HELL. One night, I was looking up something to read online and came across a book called *City of Bones* by Cassandra Clare. I began reading and became so entwined in the Shadowhunter world and the characters, who excited and inspired me.

I felt the female characters were who I used to be, and the courage and determination of Clary helped me realize my own confidence to change the situation I was in. I left with what I could carry, and I am now safe and happy with my daughter, who is almost five years old. I am forever indebted to Cassandra Clare, the magical world she envisioned, and the strong characters she created for giving me my life back. And if self-doubt starts to bubble up, I think of how I can be more like Clary, and it gives me so much peace.

Books Console Those
Who Are Broken by Life
..Barbara Kljaić..

I always admired the way the sun would fall upon the leaves and color it with light. I would look upon the stars and dream about things that never would happen, about cities that don't exist, and people who are too good for this world. I would make up stories so I could survive this, sometimes, odorous life. It would be an understatement to say I have been living in my own world since birth, but don't we all?

At the age of seven, I was "diagnosed" with dyslexia and dysgraphia, meaning I couldn't read and often misplaced numbers as well as words. Kids at school, as always, were mean about it, and it's because of their laughter that I started to hate reading. I thought, why even bother? I'm not smart enough to read. I'm not GOOD ENOUGH, like other children.

My mom, being the biggest book lover I know, was heartbroken, but she never said a word to me. I found out later that when she came back from school after speaking with my teacher, who told her how bad I was in reading, she cried. She probably thought we would never share that passion for reading but, even then, she didn't force me. It all began, at thirteen, with a book called *Delirium* by Lauren Oliver. I am so enormously thankful to her for just existing and WRITING! If it wasn't for her book, maybe I would never have started reading. My best friend, who was the rock in my life – my anchor – lent me that book whilst saying, "I think you'll like it. Give it a try!" I always heard her talking about books she had read and, in that moment, I thought, "Why not? Maybe I can enjoy books the same way she does." That period of my life was hard. I had some problems at home which made me a complete mess. Imagine a thirteen-year-old without structure or order, living in her own little world. I was lost at that point, and I think, if it weren't for books, I would've become even more so.

I'm not from America or any English-speaking country, so I read *Delirium* in my native language. But they didn't translate the sequels, so I went to the bookstore and bought them in English. And that's how I started reading in English and, later on, in German. Imagine how shocked my mom was when she found out. A girl with dyslexia, who hated books, was reading in foreign languages!

After that, I started writing as well and found the missing piece of myself in words and creation.

I had been lost, then found, and lost again. But in the end, I would always find my way back. Books were there, like a flashlight, to guide me through the dark times and redirect my passion in life. I've found that life has beauty for those who see it, and, as I began with Vincent van Gogh, I'm going to finish with him as well, "I also have nature and art and [books], and if that isn't enough, what is?" When you combine nature with books, beauty happens. The same goes for humans; when you let your "disabilities" be your stepping stones, mixing and blending them with your abilities, then miracles and magic happen!

Never underestimate yourself. Even if the world does, you mustn't be the one who knocks you down. Don't be your own worst enemy.

Books Are Anchors in the Darkness

..Charlotte Williams..

The name of this project is truly fitting. Implied by the title of my own piece, this story is centred on those shadows that creep out just before twilight, existing through the night, even when the moon is at its apex, surviving until the palette of dawn crests across the sky. Even with the light of day, however, those shadows are still there, but the pressing darkness holds no weight.

Books were, and forever will be, my light, anchoring me to hope and all that is good in the world, all that is good in me.

Personally, that dark episode took the form of depression. A suitable image, one that reflects the situation well. I was fifteen when I was first diagnosed, though I had struggled with the burden of anxiety and depression since the age of fourteen. I was relentlessly bullied by my peers at school, which resulted in me dropping out. I couldn't take it anymore.

What a relief to be free! Free from the crippling worries that kept me up at night, fearful of what the weekday would bring when I returned to the mockery, the whispers, the laughter, the humiliation.

The illusion of freedom quickly shattered.

I became lonely, confined to my house; a prisoner trapped within four walls. With each passing day, the refuge I had clung to so dearly became a warped nightmare. I couldn't face the outside world because I was so embedded in my own head. I didn't leave my house for six months straight. Not once. I had no contact with the outside world. Eventually, my mum had to take me to A&E in the early hours of the morning because my body was shutting down, and I was convinced I was dying. I was having multiple panic attacks every day. I was suicidal. I was depressed. I was hopeless.

Then I started to read.

The words and tales of others became my crutch. Straddling the planes between worlds, I felt more confident taking the necessary steps to help my recovery. I no longer felt trapped, for each time I opened a book, I was transported somewhere else. I no longer felt alone, for each time I opened a book, I journeyed alongside characters experiencing their own growth, which helped me accept and understand my circumstances. I no longer felt powerless, for each time I put pen to page, I felt in complete and utter control.

As I navigate the treacherous seas of life, words and stories keep me anchored, stopping me from floating away and getting tossed about on the waves, drowning in the murky waters. For the first time in years, something gave me a glimmer of hope. That light was ignited on a wick of words in the candle of creation.

I'm nineteen now. I'm still here, still around, still fighting my demons with the mighty Andúril, or Sting, or Longclaw, or Goldryn. Books didn't just give me hope through the recovery stages of that dark period, they have given me hope for the rest of my life. I read books. I write stories. I make sense of the world through my own tales and the tales of others.

Someday, I hope to offer others what books consistently give back to me: life.

A Light Through the Darkness

..The Reader Myth..

Reading? If you would have asked me of what importance it was when I was eight years old, I don't know what I would have answered. Following a hero through their adventure; going to the confines of every world, possible and impossible; falling in love (over and over again); taking risks even if you don't know what the outcomes will be; experiencing sadness over everyone left behind – this is the life of a reader. They do not consider books to be only physical objects; they treat them as old friends. Here are some of the lessons I learned throughout my years as a reader, and I hope everyone can experience them, at least once, in their life.

1) You decide whether you are the hero of your story, even if you do not think you have all the criteria.

2) Doing the right thing doesn't mean you are not scared, but that you do it anyway.

3) Love and hope are the saviors of our humanity.

4) Love is a miracle between two people. Something precious that has no eyes, no judgement.

5) Risks are a part of life and you have to take them to live.

6) The world is never as dark as you imagine; there is always some light everywhere, you just have to open your eyes wider.

For a reader, books are a way to experience life, or millions of them, no matter where they are. This is the power of readers and the magic of books, like a light shining through the darkness.

The Diary
of A Reader

..AlyMarie Fox..

September 2007

Dear Diary,

Today, Mommy took my sister and me to the library to return books and get new ones. We come here every Saturday, and it's my favorite thing to do because there are so many books to choose from! I'm doing the summer reading challenge so, hopefully, I will read more books than last year. And because there's no more school, I get to read as much as I want. I already know where the kids section is. I don't even wait for Mommy before going inside. While Mommy's returning our books, I get to pick out more. I'm reading *Nancy Drew*; I really like mystery books because I get to try and guess who did it. I even keep a list of clues and suspects so I remember which ones I read. I want to read them all. I want to take all of them home, read them, and go back to get more forever. I wish I could keep them all, so I can read them all over again!

Maybe one day I'll have my own library.

Anyways, time to go read!

-A

November 2009

Dear Diary,

I'm having a hard time with my friends. I don't know who they are anymore. None of them are in my class, so the only time I see them is during recess. But whenever I ask to hang out with them, they tell me they just want to hang out with each other. Then I ask the next pair of friends and they say the same thing. Is this just a coincidence?

They've been doing this every recess, always hanging out with someone else but me. Why can't I join? All they do is walk around the perimeter of the schoolyard and talk. I don't know what they talk about, but I hope it's not about me. Maybe that's why I can't hang out with them? I even asked if I could just walk with them. I promised not to say a word, but that wasn't good enough.

No one wants to play with me, so I sit all alone in the school-yard and watch everyone else having fun. My friends walk by me and, sometimes, I meet their gaze, but they don't say anything. I pretend to ignore them but once they're out of sight, I let myself cry. Maybe someone else will come and talk to me but no one ever does. Everyone seems to have someone but me.

Mommy says it'll get better. She told me to find something else to do but I don't know what. I wish I had friends.

-A

December 2009

Dear Diary,

I've started reading during recess now. Normally, I would read on the bus, but I felt risky and took my book outside even though it's cold and the time of year when it starts to snow. When I went outside, I found a remotely sunny area to sit in. Even though I was all alone, I enjoyed it. But I didn't really feel alone because I had my book to keep me company. It was like talking to a friend, except I didn't do much of the talking. Instead, I listened, but I liked it because my book had something interesting to say. I don't remember how many pages I read through the span of recess, but it felt like a lot to me, which is good because I'm a slow reader. I didn't even care when I saw my friends walk past me as usual, looking like they were flaunting their time together without me. I think they do it on purpose now, but I don't care anymore. In fact, I was glad they saw me because I wanted to show I didn't need them anymore. I've even stopped asking them to hang out with me because I know what their answer will be. If they wanted to exclude me, then I was excluding them too. I had a new friend with me, the only friend I really need.

Because books won't leave you behind. Books are always there for you, in your hands, in your heart, and in your brain.

-A

March 2011

Dear Diary,

It's déjà vu all over again. I've lost my friends. This time it's not them secretly plotting to eliminate me from the friend group (if that was even the case). No, this time they've been swallowed up by the "popular" kids. It's not that I don't like them, but they're just not the type of people I want to hang around. They're not my type; we don't have anything in common. But, one thing I don't like is, ever since my friends started hanging out with them, they've been acting different. It's like that group changed them for the worse, and I don't recognize them anymore. I thought things would be different, better even, but I guess not.

I should have known these friends wouldn't be permanent. I felt them slipping away from me, but I was always in denial. I was hopeful. I didn't realize it was actually a warning sign, foreboding what was to come. (I learned that word in English class today. Seemed appropriate to use.) Speaking of English, I'm on my fourteenth reading log! I always get a dirty look of disbelief from Mrs. when I ask for more, like she doesn't believe me, but hey, what else am I supposed to do when I have an hour of recess every day? Sit all alone and not read?

I've been inspired by the books I read to start writing my own. I've always liked the idea of making up stories and I think I might be good at it. It'd be pretty cool to write my own books and be able to read them during recess, see them in my classroom or the school library, and just think to myself, I wrote that. That's mine. I already have a book idea in my head; I'm not going to tell you just yet, but here's a hint: it's a secret.

-A

July 2012

Dear Diary,

I'm so happy because the coolest thing happened. I was home alone, humming a tune (don't ask me where I heard this tune, it kind of just came to me) and then, out of nowhere, I began to add lyrics that rhymed, right on the spot. Again, I don't know where these words came from or how they came to me... they just did. It was like a song that was stuck in my head, except I'd never heard any of it before, and as I belted the lyrics out, I made sure to write them down so I'll never forget them.

I don't know how to explain this poem (I've decided to make it a poem because I'm not much of a singer) other than it simply being perfection. Okay, it might not be that perfect, but to me it is. The words flowed so nicely out of my mouth, like someone else was speaking for me. The rhymes fit so well with each other, like pieces to a puzzle. It was like a message sent from some creative divine spirit, like Apollo or Dionysus, specifically for me. Even the subject matter perfectly related to me. I love when something creative comes to me, dare I say, so easily. It makes me feel proud and special in my own way, like I was born with writing and creative superpowers. Here's the poem, by the way:

I love to read, oh yes, I do!

I love to read, oh yes, it's true!

I love to read, you can watch me too.

Oh, I really love to read.

I read on the toilet, reading page by page,

When I'm at school or at an arcade.

You have to hear what my parents would say:

My mother says, "It has to stop."

My father says that that is enough.

My sister says "Don't read, don't read"

"Too bad I love to read!"

-A

March 2013

Dear Diary,

I want to be an author. I have never felt so sure about anything. It feels like a life or death situation, like I'll either live my life as an author and actress, or I'll die trying.

I guess I've always known that's what I wanted to do. I've been walking aimlessly along a path, knowing where it'll take me. It was instinctive, like a map programmed into the back of my head. I've been given these directions, these voices in my head, leading me to my destination. I have found my passion, my calling, and it's something I won't ignore. I can't ignore it anymore. All my meaningful memories stem from reading and writing. Every book I read, every story I wrote, every character I wanted to be were foretelling signs.

I was always a curious one when it came to books. I wanted to read every book because I saw them each as unique worlds I was willing to discover, and, with an active imagination, I wanted to produce the same material. Let me just say that I've attempted many stories with incomplete results. I tried writing a screenplay I wanted to star in when I was nine; I planned to write a mystery series at ten; I wanted to make my own picture book at six; I bought a notebook at nine where I tried rewriting the Harry Potter series by introducing a new character, which was supposed to be an alter ego of myself (I didn't even realize I was creating a fanfiction at the time). Though I do see those attempts as failures, one thing I've succeeded in doing is never giving up. Even when I have a new story idea, it may seem like I'm giving up on an old idea, but I am still trying to reach the same end goal. I have stories I want to tell, characters I want the world to meet, and adventures that have yet to be embarked on.

I want my stories to have a positive and inspiring impact on others, just like books did for me. I want to entertain people, put smiles on their faces, make them fall in love with characters, and then tear them away. I want to be just like the authors I've looked up to all my life – the ones who always leave me wanting more; the ones who come up with the most brilliant and fascinating stories; the ones who make me take a moment to think about how intelligently creative they are, making me wonder how the heck they do it.

I wish I could be just as intelligently creative. I don't know how else to explain it, but writers are like gods. They rule their own lands in the pages of their books, in the stories and characters they create with ink. They have some sort of supernatural, otherworldly powers that brings the stories to life.

It sounds a little crazy to say you want to be a god, but, in a way, that's what creators are. So, maybe, I just want to be a god in my own head. I want that power and control over my imagination. I want to bring fictional worlds and the people inside them to life.I want to be a writer. I want to be a ruler of my own lands, of my own books.

-A

May 2014

Dear Diary,

I just had the strangest dream I can't seem to get out of my mind. The thing is, I don't want to. I'm sitting on my bed right now, replaying this dream, these visions that dance around in my brain. I'm wondering how on earth this dream came to me. Is it from a movie? A book I read? I'm not sure.

I do vaguely remember listening to the *Suspiria* theme song before I went to bed. Could that be the reason? But whatever I dreamt didn't come from the movie, that's for sure. It's something I've never seen before, and I don't think there's anything out there like it. I don't know how to explain it, it just came to me. It's a gift, in more ways than one. It's a message, a calling I can't ignore.

Oh my God, did I honestly make the entire dream up on my own?!?! On a separate piece of paper, I'm writing down my dream, the pivotal main scenes that I remember. I'm switching between the both of you because I want to keep you up-to-date on the progress I'm making.

As I'm writing it, I'm coming up with ideas, plot points, background information, characters, anything that's adding a third dimension to my dream. I'm starting to see a bigger picture; I can feel it growing stronger and more powerful by the second. It's like the story is unfolding right in front of me and, with it, a purpose is passed down to me. I am the sole bearer of this story, and it's my job to pass it along, to share it with the world. And I know just the way.

-A

June 2016

Dear Diary,

I can't believe I finished writing my very first manuscript today. Yes, that actually happened. After ten years of trying to write a full-length story, I managed to finally write one in two years. The book is 800 pages (yes, that's right), but I've decided to split it into two books, which means I've already written my first two books. I've been thinking about where I'm going to end the first part and how the second one will pick up. I found a spot with a nice cliffhanger that will hopefully intrigue readers. Now that writing the book is done, my next step is to get it published. That, and writing the third book in the series (but with my luck, I'm probably going to have to split that one too).

It feels so surreal to be done writing a story from start to finish. It's one thing to plot out what happens but it's another to fully develop it into an actual narrative. I think about the journey, the late nights I spent writing, the frustration on my dad's face when he complained that all I did was sit and write, the times I shut myself out to be with the characters in my head, the endless doubt in the back of my mind, and the many tears shed while evoking a mixed variety of emotions… and this is just the beginning.

But I've come so far, the farthest I've gone in terms of writing a novel, and I don't want to stop now. I have so much faith in this child that I can't wait to see grow. I don't want it to be just a thought planted inside my head.

It will happen. I will make it happen because I have found my sole purpose in this life.

-A

January 2018

Dear Diary,

Where do I even begin?

It's the New Year and I've decided to take a look back on my life. Like, if I had to write a narrative of my life, what events would encompass my so-called journey? How would I write it? How did I even end up here? I'm taking the time to do this now, before the craziness of school starts all over again.

One thing I have to say is that I would not be where I am today without my books (this might seem silly but, since you've been with me for a long time, you know how powerful this statement is). I probably wouldn't even be studying English right now in university, trying to make a future for myself as a writer.

I cannot tell you how thankful I am to be a reader, to have had a childhood where books were so present in my life — and still are. They are my friends, they are my children, and they are my world. I can't imagine a life without books. They have shaped me into the person I am today.

So I haven't been able to read my 200 or so books in my closet (and the number keeps growing, especially after buying six more books over winter break — oops, sorry, not sorry) or even glance at my manuscript since the summer, but it doesn't mean I have stopped thinking about them or the anticipation of what these stories will bring. And I know how much I praise books always sounds a little crazy, as if they were some life-saving device that came to me in a desperate and fatal time of need, but they've saved my life in a metaphorical sense. They did things for me I will always be indebted for.

Books stayed with me when others didn't. They helped me discover my interests and passions. They inspired me to be the person I am today, and they keep inspiring me to pursue my dreams, to achieve things I want to achieve. They unleashed my creative spirit as a writer and an artist.

And, most importantly, they saved me from living in a dull, boring reality.

My life would have never been the same without books. I wouldn't have discovered this fictional universe, the door to escapism, where I can slip between fiction and reality and do what I please. I feel like an explorer sometimes, like I've discovered something magical, just for me.

I guess, all I can really say is this: I've spent all my life in one place, and though I may not sound adventurous, I have witnessed many things and felt a thousand times more pain, joy, sadness, fear, and heartbreak. I have visited more than one world and traveled through time. I've met the most amazing people and the cruelest of them all. I live through the books I read and the journeys they take me on – one day, I hope my stories can do the same for other readers like me.

-A

Escape Reality
..Krissu_LovingStories..

In my family, I was always the loud, obnoxious kid. I was never out of energy; I was clearly happy. Up until I hit puberty, became very self-conscious, and moved to a new middle school. I was pretty shy and didn't make a lot of friends. Middle school was the lowest point in my life. My creativity was low, I fell into a pit of doubt, and always felt unsafe. I was moody, sad, and questioned my existence. I hated how I felt every time I thought about the future, and it killed me to know I had no purpose. I couldn't really appreciate middle school life without drowning. It was in my last few weeks of eighth grade that I picked up a book and felt different. It was a children's book, but I didn't care. Reading felt refreshing and assured me I was safe. From that point on, I continued reading more and more. Although I had my low times, I would get that same book and, once again, feel the childhood giddiness of living in worlds that were made by creators, with a reality that was different and special. And I want to join those worlds – to escape reality into one that welcomes me.

Discovery

..Ana Paula Camacho Pérez..

Insecurities constitute one of the most hidden secrets of human nature. They're the foundation of the many walls and barriers we build around ourselves to keep the world from finding out who we really are. Because, apparently, vulnerability is a human calamity, and we can't afford falling into it. Humans will do anything in their power to bury them deep inside their souls, without noticing it makes them become another dull, blended shadow in the materialistic, unsubstantial world where "I'm okay" has become the only acceptable answer.

For me, insecurities started with something quite ironic: words. From an early age, I was unable to formulate words of my own, not because of incapability, but because fear and a strong ache filled my stomach every time my lips tried to produce any type of sound. This, as expected, led me to live in a state of unwanted isolation, loneliness, and lack of self-acceptance with no integration to the developing society around me.

Some believed I didn't understand them, others that I was unwilling to try, or they simply turned their backs on me. What they never dared to reflect on was how, even with my mouth shut, I was still unable to shut the dark feelings they were causing to arise deep inside my heart.

I found total comfort in only one person: my grandmother. Inside a new wooden cupboard, she kept three enormous books whose contents I was so intrigued to uncover. Hours before dawn came, my hands, sweating from curiosity, would stretch to reach the stories I yearned to discover. Still, without the capability of reading, I would ask my grandmother to read them out loud over and over again. Little by little, I learned every single word that resonated from her lips, every one of them whispering stories that felt as real as myself. I only dreamt of one thing from that moment: being able to discover those tales by myself.

Little did I know, I would soon be embarking on a lifetime journey. I remember it quite clearly: my dark brown shoes, ironed skirt, and neatly combed pigtails. However, I mostly remember the item I tightly held between my hands: my first book. That day, as usual, the morning bell rang. I sat on the crowded playground, letting the children's screams surround my silent self. With my little fingers, I gently brushed the pages whose story would change my life forever. My first words, my first journey, the first time I didn't feel alone:

"Chapter One: The Wrong Door. This is a story about something that happened long ago when your grandfather was a child. It is a very important story because it shows how all the comings and goings between our own world and the land of Narnia first began."

- C.S. Lewis

In Dreams

..J.D. Netto..

I was always the oddball growing up in Brazil. While the other boys were outside playing soccer, I was cooped up in my room, my face often buried in a book. If I wasn't reading, I was drawing comics or plotting out elaborate stories while playing with my action figures.

For as long as I can remember, I've been passionate about storytelling. Whether it was books, movies, or music, I was absolutely enthralled by the power of art. Though criticized during those years for my lack of interest in what people deemed normal, I was completely fascinated by fictional universes.

My family moved to America in 2000, and I clearly remember the day my mother took me to a thrift store where I found an old copy of *Jurassic Park* by Michael Crichton and *The Adventures of Huckleberry Finn* by Mark Twain. I didn't even know *Jurassic Park* was a book until that day.

I remember reading those stories and thinking: *I have found my own group of misfits!* My love for the make-believe grew stronger with every word I read.

In my head, I was always creating something; a monster, a warrior, a dragon. I was always off fighting some battle or riding a horse with my sword in hand. But it wasn't until 2002 that I felt completely sane. During that year, my friend introduced me to Tolkien's masterpiece, *The Lord of the Rings*. Yes, I had heard about the first movie, but at the time, I wasn't that interested.

Reading those books made me understand the power of creativity and how it can inspire one to be better. Though young at the time, I saw my own struggles reflected in the journey of each character. I finally realized there was a purpose for the monsters and characters living in my head.

Tolkien was the inspiration for me to discover other works of fantasy. Narnia and Harry Potter came right after! After living one thousand lives, I was eventually inspired to write my own tale. Had it not been for the authors who so boldly shared their private worlds with the universe, I would not have been bold enough to share my own.

Reading taught me to stop questioning the ideas in my head and simply trust them, no matter how wild. I learned to take every comment and situation, and turn them into creative fuel.

There's purpose in the journey. It requires courage to get to the destination. Many give up on the way. Reading taught me to be one of the few who don't.

Not Alone

..Annaellen..

After I started reading on a daily basis, I learned things about myself. I was nine or ten at the time, and you were considered a nerd if you read a lot. I continued reading because I loved it and didn't care, at that age, how others saw me.

Later on, I started to feel a bit left out at school, but with books, I never felt like I was alone. I could dive into a book and feel better. Reading really helped me though the hardest parts of my youth. I lost a trusted friend and was feeling out of place, but thanks to books and the words in them, I knew I was going to be fine.

With books, I never felt alone. It was okay to be a bookworm, and it was okay to be me.

And now that I have come out stronger, I dare to tell people I love reading. I am a book nerd, but so what? So are millions of others. I love reading, and that's what matters most.

#ProudBookworm

Reading Through the Grief

..Abby Moeller..

I was sixteen.

I was a junior in high school.

And things were going okay enough.

Yes, there were some ups and downs and a heaping amount of stress, but I was surviving. I was reading all the time, and not just for my classes. Books were one of my closest friends, and with every free opportunity I had, my nose was shoved between the pages. They gave me peace and serenity. They offered escape from the real world and the problems that hid and strived there. I thrived in books, and I was also starting to wield words and craft my own stories. Bonding over books was how I met my best friend. Where would we be if books and our high school book club hadn't brought us together, V?

Words and I went hand in hand. (And still do.)

But, suddenly, my aunt passed. A young woman with a five-month-old baby. It was a shock. (It still is.) It was crushing. It ruined everything. Having breakdowns throughout the school day became a new norm.

A week later, another member of my family passed, my great-grandmother. That was another crack to my sanity.

I was hardly moving by that point.

SATs and AP exams were coming up, and I barely had the motivation to take them. I lost all interest in succeeding in school or keeping myself together. Nothing seemed real, to be honest.

But then, a book seemed to open up my heart and mind.

The Bell Jar.

I found myself diving into the words of that book and never wanting to come out. Plath's novel helped me evaluate and recognize the grief and struggles I was having as a result of those deaths. That book helped me heal, to grow. To find peace and a little bit of solace that helped me move on each and every day. I was starting to accept the facts and truths I had been so desperate to ignore, to squash down despite the deep heartache that grew with every breath and heartbeat. That book is now one of my absolute favorites. I cherish it more than anything sometimes.

That wasn't the first time books brought me a small peace from my grief. It was middle school, I was about twelve or thirteen, and I had lost my great-grandfather and my cat. This cat was my everything; I had grown up alongside her, so it was a staggeringly traumatic event. I remember getting angry at a Ray Bradbury documentary in English class where he had a cat walking along his shoulders. "It wasn't fair his cat was alive and mine wasn't," was my reasoning. I struggled then, too. But books helped me fall away from the pain of reality and find peace. Words blanketed me and gave me an escape that was worth everything. That will never change; books have given me a second home. It seems grief has a clever way of always finding me, but what grief doesn't know is I have books by my side to help me keep living, loving, reading, and remembering those I have lost.

I still hurt.

I still miss them.

But because of books, I can live.

I can breathe.

I can get up each morning and think about how much I love my family, living and dead, and not crumble to my knees, a sobbing wreck. (Though there are still tears from time to time.)

Books are family now. I feel safe and at home in between the pages. I drink down words like water and grow from the endless stories I absorb.

Books saved me from falling down the rabbit hole of grief, and I hope others will find the same savior in them as I did.

Grief still has a home in my heart, but cracked book spines have a stronger presence in comparison.

Breathe In
the Words and Be

..Emilie Messavussu..

A drop of rain pelted my face.

The breeze ruffled my locks, tickling the side of my face and neck.

The sky grew darker and the smell of rain more evident, a promise of a storm.

Voices roared in the distance, near my ears, but my mind was plugged into the book in my hands. I was there, but not really. Battle cries rang, mixing with the rain. Screams filled the air. Laughter. Pain. Love. Loss. Happiness. Joy. Sadness, and so much more...

A great read is capable of many wonders for the mind, body, and soul. It hypnotizes and arises things through the imagination that can't be explained. Imagination's ability was and always will be persuasive and informative – whether the information provided is deemed plausible or not.

The darkness didn't swallow the cries and screams. The metal gates were forced shut, people shouting for cover, war tanks drove through the dusty ground of our front door, havoc reigned without an end in sight. Mama held me closer to her chest. My eyes burned. Papa called that night, but he was an ocean away. His words of safety were useless as the tear gas thrown over our home continued to torment my eyes. I was around six or seven years old. Lomé, Togo, West Africa was my home, but after all that, my mother, sisters, and I moved in with my father. I call Chicago, Illinois my home now, for nearly thirteen years actually.

I was an outsider. I barely spoke English. My French and Mina had no use in a classroom that mainly spoke English. My accent was different. I could understand a few words spoken to me. But, even then, I couldn't respond. I was bullied; physically, emotionally, verbally... over where I came from and for just being me. The grownups in my life didn't offer the help I needed. I felt low, nearly resorting to cutting away the pain. I was around seven, and I felt that way for nine years after.

I hated reading and writing – with a burning passion. Maybe it was because, at the time, I barely spoke English. Then I was given a book called *Percy Jackson & the Olympians: The Lightning Thief* by Rick Riordan. I was hooked and continued to read the rest of the books till I finished the series. I loved it, not even aware I had tossed my hatred for books out the window. I read and read, diving into stories to sate the hunger inside me. I wanted more, and the words in those books were my cure. I didn't care that I was still an outcast. With every book, I became someone with a purpose. With every book, I grew more confident in myself. With every book, I had a goal I wanted to accomplish.

If you would've told that young, African seven-year-old girl who first came to the United States that she'd find the confidence and determination to succeed, I'd never have believed you. Because of my love of books, I'm proudly pursuing an English major with a minor in marketing; my goal is to become an editor at a publishing house. I may be a sophomore now, my head still partially in the clouds, but that's the beauty of it. Even as I continue to grow, reaching to accomplish my goals, I still want to live a creative life. A life I'd never have thought I could pursue if I hadn't dove into the beauty of reading.

Not only do I love reading, but writing has become my drive to continue as well. Reading not only saved my life, but gave me a purpose. You can live, but if you're not *really* living, what do you gain from it all? Live the best creative life you possibly can. Books, as you can see, can alter the lives of its readers.

43

Paper Wings

..Rey R...

I need reading as much as I need oxygen. I need the stories, the characters, and the sweet release from reality. I have truly lived a thousand lives, and I know a thousand more await me hidden between the pages of books. I have gone to space, traveled the world, felt joy and heart-wrenching sadness. I have made incredible friends and lost them too. And I love it all.

But what I love most is the magic. Some days, I can hardly stand the white noise that is reality. How can I, when I have fought dragons, visited castles, flown, and traveled through time?

Reading is a long-needed breath. A break. An opportunity to shed your skin and become someone else. Reading is the much-needed escape from the tediousness of real life. Sometimes, I think I'd rather be doing something extraordinary, like one of my favorite characters, than study for a topic I won't remember in a few days. But we only have this life, and so we must take what we can from it. We don't get to save the world, but we can do it through the pages of books. And it is wonderful.

Lifesaver

..Yesenia M. Collado...

Going into my freshman year of high school, I moved to a new city and school away my friends. I thought I would be the center of attention when I started this new high school, but the truth was no one cared. I had no friends whatsoever for most of freshman year. I also discovered who my real friends were, the people who have been there for me since middle school. And I am so thankful to them for staying rather than leaving like the rest. Since I had no friends at my new high school, I had to eat lunch alone. I got really depressed and wanted to kill myself, but reading gave me a reason to keep living. More specifically, *Empire of Storms* by Sarah J. Maas and, wow, that series changed my life. I knew I couldn't die because I had to know what happened in the next book. So yes, reading has really saved my life. It made the suicidal thoughts go away and, with it, came the dawning realization there's more to life than just living and dying; there are entire worlds out there yet to be discovered that are held in books and imaginations.

45

The Things I Couldn't Say

..Laura Diaz Arce..

There are only two things I avoid telling people. One: I rarely indulge myself in talking about well, my real feelings. And two: I have yet to tell people about the things I felt as a child. Let me tell you that I have become an expert at these things. I can deflect better than Wonder Woman can ricochet bullets with her gauntlets. It is rather annoying for my therapists.

Here I am. Doing both.

What in the world am I doing?

Telling you, reader, I suppose, about the way I was when I was young. Telling you about how I felt.

When I was a child I was afraid. All. The. Time. Not just normal fear either, consistent horror-movie-esque fear that permeated my existence.

And what was I afraid of? Honestly, probably everything. Growing up poor, there is a lot of anxiety that permeates a household. There's scarcity and insecurity that accompanies poverty and that can be felt even when you're young.

I was also frightened of my body, of what it was. I wanted so desperately to be thin, for instance, that I had developed anorexia by the first grade and was repeatedly hospitalized for it through elementary school. My fear of food, of being fat, made me destroy my system.

But it was more than that. I had difficulty going places, being around people. I developed sleep problems early; too scared to close my eyes in the dark. The TV had to be on at night or else the anxiety would crush me.

All this fear drowned me as a child, and even worse was that I was too afraid to express it. It's not something that's fully left me, even as I've grown up.

Books didn't save me per say, but reading did ease the burden. Reading, especially reading fantasy, allowed me to imagine a version of me that wasn't afraid. I could be someone else, somewhere else, and I could overcome the worst of it.

Reading gave me the blueprints to a new personality. Even if I didn't feel brave or confident, I could pretend. I could present myself as someone who was. Someone that wasn't cowering under a heavy cloak of fear and insecurity. Little by little I built myself from words on a page.

Then I got the notion to start telling my own stories. As easily as words flowed into me, they have come spilling back out in spurts. Now I build fantasies for other people. I'm still frightened, all the time, but stories prop me up. Sometimes I'm able to give up my fears in favor of the power and the unbridled joy that comes with storytelling.

Books built me into my own hero, brave enough to face the worst of it.

To be the first to receive news
and updates, follow the
Saved by the Page movement!

SavedbythePage

www.SavedbythePage.com

we're all
misfits
saved by the page